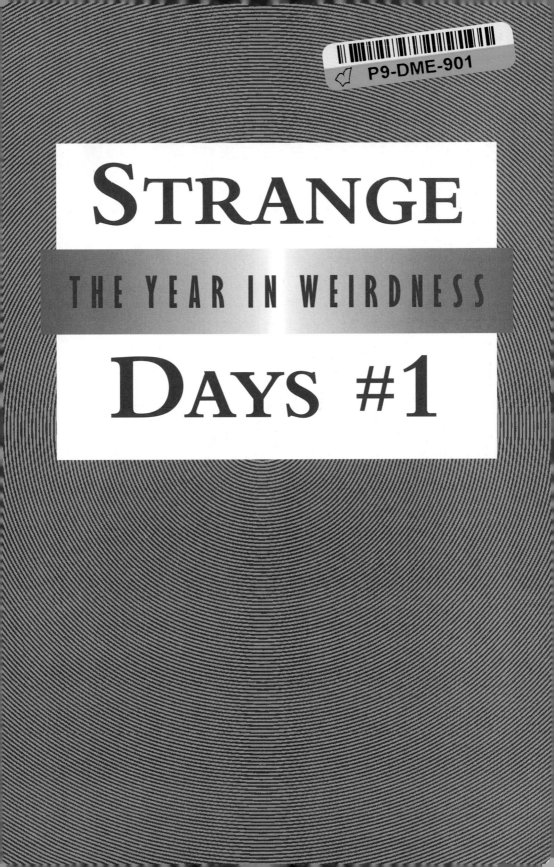

STRANGE

THE YEAR IN WEIRDNESS

DAYS #1

STRANGE

THE YEAR IN WEIRDNESS

DAYS #1

BY THE EDITORS OF
FORTEAN TIMES

CADER BOOKS

ANDREWS AND MCMEEL
A UNIVERSAL PRESS SYNDICATE COMPANY
KANSAS CITY

Thank you for buying this Cader Book—we hope you enjoy it. And thanks as well to the store that sold you this, and the hardworking sales rep who sold it to them. It takes a lot of people to make a book (even a strange one). Here are some of the many who were instrumental:

EDITORIAL:
Rufus Griscom, Heidi Herman, Jake Morrissey, Dorothy O'Brien, Regan Brown

DESIGN:
Charles Kreloff

COPY EDITING/PROOFING:
Karen Martin, Brian Bendlin

PRODUCTION:
Carol Coe, Cathy Kirkland

LEGAL:
Renee Schwartz, Esq.

FORTEAN CONSULTANTS:
Mike Dash, Bob Rickard, Joe McNally

And thanks to Bill Barker for permission to use the Schwa symbol. To purchase Schwa products, write Box 6064, Reno NV 89513 or visit:
http://www.theschwacorporation.com

If you would like to share any thoughts about this book, or are interested in other books by us, please write to:

Cader Books
38 E. 29 Street
New York, NY, 10016

Or visit our cool new web site:
http://www.caderbooks.com

Library of Congress
Cataloging-in-Publication Data

Strange days #1 : the year in weirdness / by the editors of Fortean times. — 1st ed.
       p.   cm.
     ISBN: 0-8362-1499-4 (pbk.)
     1. Curiosities and wonders.
2. Parapsychology.   I. Fortean times.
AG243.S835   1996   96-12712
031.02—dc20   CIP

April 1996

First edition
10 9 8 7 6 5 4 3 2 1

CONTENTS

....

THE HUMAN WORLD
....

RECREATIONAL AMPUTATION, THE ILLINOIS ENEMA BANDIT, AND OTHER ODDITIES...

SCHWASCAR AWARDS

THE ANIMAL WORLD

EXPLODING WHALES, HERMAPHROGOATS,
AND OTHER ODDITIES...

THE NATURAL WORLD

SWARMINGS, METEORITE CAR CRASHES, AND OTHER ODDITIES...

THE PARANORMAL WORLD

BLEEDING SCULPTURES, POLTERGEIST BURGLARS,
AND OTHER ODDITIES...

WEIRD STUFF HAPPENS

There's no getting away from that fact, no matter how much stuffy scientists may resent it and narrow-minded people revile it. Weird stuff happens and is reported in *Fortean Times*.

We subtitle ourselves "The Journal of Strange Phenomena" because we are a forum for recording and discussing extraordinary experiences, observations, behavior, things, creatures or beliefs. They are strange because they are not previously known or expected. We don't use the word "paranormal" because we'd have to first agree on what "normal" means, and it's this kind of dogma that starts wars. Our stories, compiled from newspaper reports around the world as well as our own investigations, are the exceptions that don't prove any rules.

What kinds of things do we mean by "strange phenomena"? Well, since we began publishing in 1973, we have learned to expect the unexpected. Examples of what the universe (some folk think "multiverse" would be a better term) throws at us might be unexplained disappearances of people; spontaneous human combustion; UFO-related phenomena; lake monsters and sea serpents; lights seen on the moon; stigmatic wounds; hoaxes and mass panics; rains of stones or animals from the skies; wolf children and wild men; visions, levitations and other alleged miracles; animals that shouldn't be there; spontaneous natural images; new species; and fancy-dress crimes. As you'll see in this selection of stories, we pay attention to the humorous, the whimsical, and the dark side of things as well as to serious paradigm-changing discoveries.

So, why "Fortean"? We are named in honor of a strange Albanian. The eponymous Charles Fort (1875–1932) was born in Albany, New York. He had a passion for data and stories that did not fit in with the accepted explanations of the day. He spent most of his life in the main libraries in New York and London amassing a vast database of notes which found their way into four books; the first and most famous being *The Book of the Damned*, published in 1919. Today, *Fortean Times* gathers similar materials using the Internet, computers and a growing network of readers who participate by sending us news clippings.

Charles Hoy Fort (1874–1932)

Fort observed how people argued for and against various theories, facts and kinds of phenomena according to their own beliefs rather than the rules of evidence. Scientists were no exception. He was appalled by the way that any datum that did not fit one scientist's view, or the collective paradigm, was systematically ignored, suppressed, discredited or explained away (which is quite a different thing from explaining something).

Fort called such rejected data "the

damned" because they were excommunicated by a science that behaved like a religion. Famous examples of such "priestly" rejections are the notion of fossils (scorned by Voltaire); meteorites (Lavoisier told the French Academy of Sciences in 1769 that only peasants believed that stones fell from the sky because there were no stones in the sky, thus delaying the acceptance of meteorites until 1803); space flight (condemned by a senior British scientist in the 1930s as "utter bosh!"); and so on.

Fort attracted the attention of many of the literary stars of the day because he had dared the unusual—a criticism of the practice of science couched in eccentric but dramatic and witty prose. In 1942, Ben Hecht (who wrote the screenplays for classic films like *The Front Page*) hailed Fort as "Apostle of the Exception, Keeper of Ghosts, Observer of Secret Rays, Avenger of Forgotten Theories, Lost Causes and Strayed Comets; Jocular Priest of the Improbable and Demonstrator of Idiocies."

But Fort—and by extension, we Forteans—are not the enemies of science we are said to be. Historically, most cultures have had an appreciation of anomalies that we have lost, including some framework in which to study or interpret them. For example, priests in rural Scandinavia in the late medieval period were obliged to report to their bishops anything contrary to the "natural order." Their surviving chronicles are treasure troves of sea serpent sightings, falls of mice and fish, battles between armies of animals and other unusual phenomena.

It is not without significance that these weirdness-watchers—from aboriginal animists to Greek oracles and Chinese cosmologists—all developed a similar philosophy, seeing evidence of the indivisibility of the universe, every part of which is connected with every other part as though it were a single organism. The flaw in modern scientific thinking, thought Fort, is in its attempt to define, divide and separate. "Every science is a mutilated octopus," he wrote. "If its tentacles were not clipped to stumps, it would feel its way into disturbing contacts."

All we are saying is that the scientific world view cannot be the only valid explanation of the experienced world. Fort—who was not a credulous man—urged us not to invest our energy in belief but to hold ideas, facts, theories and explanations lightly, until something better came along that explained more of the phenomena than before. This is what good scientists do, too.

Though still largely unknown, Charles Fort had a profound influence on modern culture. Thirty years before the term "flying saucer" was coined during Kenneth Arnold's sighting in 1947, Fort had collected notes on lights and objects seen dancing, speeding and hovering in the skies. He wondered whether they were alien vehicles ("super-constructions," he called them) or unknown forms of natural phenomena. He also noticed that sightings came in "flaps," as exemplified by the mystery "airships" across America in 1896–97. Fort's speculations went further. He anticipated the idea of "ancient astronauts" by over 40 years, imagining that the strange vitrified forts of Scotland had been destroyed in some ancient space war. "I think we're property," he wrote, exploring the idea that perhaps humans were being developed as livestock, or were sitting tenants in some cosmic rent-war. But, Fort supposed, if there were aliens with advanced technologies, they might be able to project images of themselves onto Earth . . . or they might have appeared on Earth in person in earlier times and been taken for apparitions or demons.

Fort coined the term "teleportation," which he saw as a primary source for the distribution of matter, objects and life forms throughout the universe.

The word is now synonymous with the idea of instantaneous transportation from one place to another as depicted in *Star Trek*. If, Fort speculated, the teleportive force could come under human control, then poltergeist phenomena, levitation, bilocation or psychokinesis could perhaps occur consciously. Many of these ideas were seized upon by leading American science fiction and fantasy writers—such as Robert Heinlein, Theodore Sturgeon, James Blish, Charles Harness, August Derleth and Philip Jose Farmer, some of whom were also members of the Fortean Society—and thus passed into the collective image bank.

Today, oddity reports are mostly absent from the scientific journals where Fort found them. They have been relegated to the category of small filler paragraphs in newspapers, written inaccurately and scornfully, for laughs. But quite ordinary people continue to have extraordinary experiences and see extraordinary things. Their natural home is *Fortean Times*, where we do not judge on the basis of preconceived ideas about what is impossible. For us, the extraordinary is just another day at the office.

The stories presented in this volume were published in *Fortean Times* during 1995—generally referred to in the text as "this year"—although you are bound to find some accounts of 1994 weird-ness and occasional references to earlier events. All dates that do not include a year refer to 1995. As we believe in noting our sources wherever possible, you will find an abbreviated list of references at the back of the book.

This volume uses the categories of our famed Strangeness Index (which begins on page XIV) as its organizing principle. In the best scientific tradition, data which did not fit into the available categories were generally ignored or shoehorned into one anyway. Much of the boxed material throughout the book reflects new trends in abnormal phenomena which became evident in the course of sifting though a year's worth of Fortean clippings. We have also introduced a new feature here: the "Schwascar" award. "Schwa," the name for the omnipresent alien graphic created by artist Bill Barker in 1992, has come to signify the enigmatic or abnormal. The award is presented for exceptionally weird occurrences.

We have been recording strange phenomena for 22 years, but we are not jaded or cynical. The sheer variety and strangeness of the stories we see every day is a constant delight—a delight we want to share with you.

BOB RICKARD
FOUNDER AND EDITOR
FORTEAN TIMES
JANUARY 1996

1996 STRANGENESS INDEX

The *Fortean Times* Strangeness Index, our legendary barometer of the bizarre, is an attempt to reflect the overall weirdness of the world. Sadly, we cannot accurately measure weirdness itself (yet); however, we are in an excellent position to measure how weird the world is *reported* to be, simply by examining the stories that have been sent to, and have appeared in, *Fortean Times*.

In order to quantify worldwide weirdness as accurately as possibly, we have broken down abnormal phenomena into the 34 representative categories below. Every year we compare the number of bizarre incidents reported in each category to the previous year. Increases are designated by up arrows, decreases by down arrows, and no change by horizontal arrows.

Though we generally rely upon our own archives of newspaper clippings and research in assessing weirdness levels, a spectacular increase in outside reporting on a topic which wasn't included in *Fortean Times*— the spin-offs from the Oklahoma bombing, for example, which falls under Cults and Conspiracies—was included in our index calculations.

WORLDWIDE WEIRDNESS FLUCTUATIONS IN 1995

THE HUMAN WORLD

ANTIQUITIES ↘

STRANGE BEHAVIOR →

CULTS & CONSPIRACIES ↘

DEATHS & SUICIDES ↗

GENIUS & DISCOVERY →

HOAXES & PANICS ↘

INEPTITUDE & STUPIDITY ↗

THE ANIMAL WORLD

OUT-OF-PLACE ANIMALS ↗

ATTACKS BY ANIMALS →

ATTACKS ON ANIMALS ↘

SWARMINGS ↘

NEW SPECIES FOUND ↗

MASS DEATHS ↗

MANIMALS →

WATER MONSTERS ↗

THE NATURAL WORLD

CROP CIRCLES ↘

DISASTERS, NATURAL
& MAN-MADE ↗

BIOLOGICAL & MEDICAL ↗

EPIDEMICS & ILLNESS ↗

FALLS FROM THE SKY ↘

SPONTANEOUS HUMAN
COMBUSTION ↘

METEOROLOGICAL
SUPERLATIVES ↗

GEOPHYSICAL ACTIVITY ↘

THE PARANORMAL WORLD

PSYCHICAL PHENOMENA ↘

PROPHECIES ↘

APPARITIONS ↘

IMAGES ↗

BAD LUCK ↘

GOOD LUCK ↘

MIRACLES ↗

POLTERGEISTS →

UFOs ↗

CLOSE ENCOUNTERS
& ALIEN ABDUCTIONS ↘

PARANORMAL EXPERIENCES ↘

Taking into account the ups and downs noted above, we have calculated that the world was 1.5% less weird last year than the year before.

How did we arrive at this?

When the original Index was created in 1992 each category was assigned a baseline value of 100. Starting with a total baseline value of 3,400 in 1992, the Index rose to 3,520 in 1993, fell to 3,450 in 1994, and has now slipped back to its original value of 3,400.

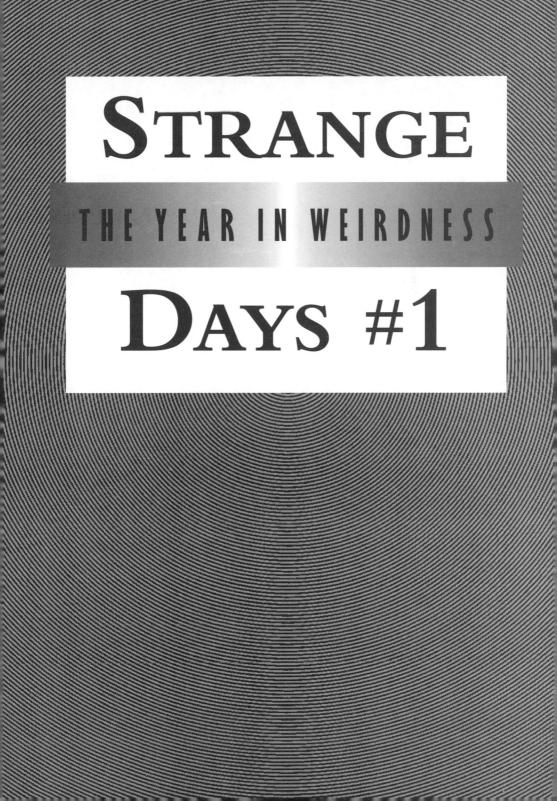

STRANGE

THE YEAR IN WEIRDNESS

DAYS #1

THE
HUMAN
WORLD

THE HUMAN WORLD

Anewly discovered tree-dwelling tribe, a rash of accordion stabbings in Germany, a French lawyer suing his six alter-egos—any news of interesting human behavior is game in this section.

The main trend in the human world this year seemed to be increasingly stupid and violent behavior. Cults and Conspiracies were well up, with the Aum Shinri Kyo gas attack on Tokyo and the Oklahoma City Bombing (though not recorded here, they registered an increase in our Strangeness Index). Hoaxes and Panics were down, although Ineptitude and Stupidity were up. People may have become too stupid to play good hoaxes any more—could this have something to do with the increase in Deaths and Suicides?

ANTIQUITIES

PRAISE HIM FROM WHOM ALL SHORTHAND FLOWS

Sir Isaac Pitman, inventor of the Pitman's phonetic shorthand system, has been officially recognized as a Hindu god.

An old photograph of Sir Isaac, complete with bindu (the dot on the forehead), now appears among the portraits of gods and goddesses at the Stenographer's Guild in Madras, placed there apparently on behalf of the thousands of Indian clerks who feel they owe their jobs to Pitman's invention.

Great-grandson Peter Pitman is delighted that flowers are offered up to his ancestor every Friday. He feels that the fact that Pitman was a vegetarian and teetotaler may have helped endear him to the Hindu community.

"He became a vegetarian only when his wife asked him to kill a chicken for lunch," he says. "He cut its head off and it ran round the kitchen minus its head. He never ate meat again."

PROPHYLACTIC TACTICS

Naval historian Peer Kuewar has solved the mystery of the 2,000 condoms found aboard the Nazi submarine U534, which worked out to nearly 40 condoms per crew member. They were to be blown up and left to float on the surface to confuse enemy radar.

WELL OF HOPE

An ancient well on the English Isle of Sheppey, in the Thames estuary, could again become a place of pilgrimage.

Reputed to have curative properties, the well was originally inside Minster Abbey, founded in 670 by the Queen of Kent, later Saint Sexburga, making it the third oldest abbey site in England. Sheppey Archeological Society hopes that by the end of the year it will have raised the last $3,750 it needs to uncap the well, restore it fully and build a roof over it.

The archeologist who found this ancient fertility symbol in an English well promptly conceived a daughter.

Southern Water has already donated $1,500.

The well was excavated in 1990–91, and drinkable water was discovered more than 31 feet down. A curious fertility symbol was brought to light from the mud at 40 feet. It was a metal image, repeated in beeswax, of a three-headed pregnant woman, conceivably representing Maid, Mother and Crone—or Spring, Summer and Winter. This might be evidence of pagan worship that predates Sexburga's abbey. The well became known as "The Well of the Triple-Headed Goddess."

Sharon White gave birth to daughter Emily in June 1991, nine months after Ian, her archaeologist husband, touched the fertility symbol while excavating the well. She had suffered four miscarriages and specialists had been unable to discover the problem. In early 1993, the couple had a second daughter.

"Because of what I have been through," said Sharon, "I would hate to build up anyone's hopes; but if they opened the well, it would give people a chance."

HOLY GRAIL TAKEN FOR A SPIN

An agate chalice kept in Valencia Cathedral in Spain, where it is regarded as the original Holy Grail used by Christ at the Last Supper, made an 800-mile excursion in a bus on June 18, 1994, accompanied by 20 busloads of pilgrims.

First it went to the cathedral at Jaca, capital of Huesca province, for a mass to

PECULIAR PRESS

GOD HOLDS UP TRAFFIC
Bedfordshire (England),
April 10, 1994

MISSING PENIS FORCES POLICE TO REOPEN CASE
Bangkok Post,
April 11, 1994

EVIL SPIRITS CLASH WITH HOLY GHOST
The Monitor (Uganda),
April 12, 1994

commemorate the death in 994 of King Sancho II, a Grail devotee. Then it was taken to the San Juan de la Pesa monastery, now deserted, where it was the focal point of an all-night vigil. It was returned to Valencia the next day.

The Civil Guard was mobilized to escort the relic, which has a pedigree dating back to the year 285. In that

IT'S ABOUT TIME

❧ Polite Japanese risk death by bowing. At least 24 Tokyo residents have died in the last five years while bowing to each other. Five fell under trains after head butts, seven died in curbside and escalator collisions and many more have been injured in revolving doors. The city has introduced safe "Greetings Zones."

❧ The Turkish religious affairs directorate, Diyanet, has distributed a booklet rebutting over 60 beliefs attributed to Mohammed. These included: biting a tombstone to cure toothache; cramming earth down a child's throat to prevent bedwetting; and hiding a child's umbilical cord in a mosque to guarantee a career as a famous scientist.

❧ On March 16, the Mississippi House of Representatives finally ratified the 13th Amendment to the constitution, abolishing slavery. The state failed to ratify the amendment in 1865 because legislators were angry that they had not been reimbursed for the value of freed slaves.

❧ Comedian Jacob Haugaard became Denmark's first independent Member of Parliament in the general election on September 21. His campaign promises included better weather, shorter lines, tailwinds for cyclists and the right of men to be impotent.

year, Saint Lorenzo, one of the seven deacons of the Roman Church serving Pope Sixtus II, was executed for his faith by the Emperor Valerian. Before being roasted to death on a gridiron, he managed to pass the Grail to a follower, a young Spaniard serving in the Roman legions.

The soldier gave the chalice to his parents in Huesca, who passed it to the Benedictine monks of San Juan de la Pesa monastery, where it remained until taken to Valencia by King Alfonso V in 1430, after which its travels were over—until this year. The agate quarry in Syria where the chalice was allegedly made was in use during Christ's lifetime. The base of the chalice was added in the 10th century, encrusted with gold and precious stones.

According to a contrary legend, the Grail was buried on Glastonbury Tor by Joseph of Arimathea in the year 60 and became the object of the Arthurian quest. Rival modern claimants to the Grail include Genoa, Italy, where the cathedral museum contains a bowl said to have been brought back by the Crusaders.

TREE TRIBES CHARTED

People from the village of Somo in Irian Jaya, near Papua New Guinea, have sighted a primitive tribe living in treehouses, according to local elder Arnold Tangkudung.

Mr. Tangkudung said they were naked and he believed the tribe had no previous contact with the outside world and still practiced cannibalism. The last cannibalistic, tree-living tribe to be discovered, the Mek, was found in 1974 in the same area. There have been several unconfirmed sightings since.

Meanwhile, in the Amazon rainforest, another unknown Indian tribe has been discovered. A Brazilian government expedition came across a man and a woman in the western state of Rondonia in early September. The Indians, who carried bows and arrows, were near two huts which had corn, bananas and yams planted close by. There are thought to be other uncharted tribes in the region, about 2,400 miles northwest of Rio.

SAY WHAT?

🌑 A man on a giant inflatable lobster rescued a young girl drifting out to sea on a set of blow-up teeth off Dover, England. The coast guard launched two lifeboats, but the lobster reached the girl first.

🌑 Police in Germany are baffled by a wave of accordion stabbings. A person or persons unknown have broken into 11 Bonn music stores and plunged butcher's knives into the instruments.

🌑 From *Churchdown Parish Magazine* in Gloucestershire, England: "Would the congregation please note that the bowl at the back of the church labeled 'For the Sick' is for monetary donations only."

🌑 A varnished human hand found in a car glove compartment by a mechanic in Austin, Texas, was "handed down as a family heirloom" and was not evidence of foul play. Originally owned by an anatomy professor, it now belongs to his granddaughter.

STRANGE BEHAVIOR

MOWER ODYSSEY

When Alvin Straight, 73, heard that his 80-year-old brother Henry had had a stroke, he knew he had to visit him. Since, like his brother, Alvin can't see well enough to get a driving license and is too independent to let anyone else drive, he bought a John Deere lawn mower and a 10-foot trailer for gasoline, clothes, food and camping gear. On July 5 he set off on the 240-mile trek from his home in Laurens, Iowa, to Henry's place near Blue River, Wisconsin.

In mid-July, Straight made it to Charles City 111 miles away, where he ran out of money. He camped out until his next welfare check came through in August; and set off again. On good days, he averaged about 5 mph for 10 hours. His mower broke down two miles from his brother's house on August 15, 1994. A farmer helped him push it the rest of the way. He planned to stay through the winter, but said he might head home after a month—on his lawn mower.

WINDSURFING TO FREEDOM

A Cuban jet ski and windsurf instructor surfed his way across 110 miles of shark-infested sea. Eugenio Maderal, 21, who taught at the Varadero beach resort, landed at Marathon on the upper Florida Keys on the night of February 8, 1994, nine hours after deciding to take advantage of strong winds to escape life under Castro. He had no food or water and wore only a pair of shorts. Maderal was encouraged by the fact that his friend Lester Moreno had surfed to America in 1990. Moreno, then 17, was picked up by a freighter 30 miles from Key West. He now works with computers.

EXPLOSIVE FOOTWEAR

These women's sandals, in jazzy neon colors, are part of the A-Bomb line created by Mode et Jacomo, a Tokyo design company. It also produces A-Bomb bags and fashion accessories.

A Japanese design firm named a fashion line after the atomic bomb, thinking it was "cute."

"A-Bomb stands for atomic bomb," said Miyuki Kamiya, the firm's public relations officer, "but I was also told that it could mean 'cute' in English." She had heard that some stores in Hiroshima had expressed reluctance to market A-Bomb items, but she didn't know if any retailers had actually refused to do so.

CRIMINALS NAIL THEMSELVES

Prisoners in Romania are hammering nails into their skulls with metal tea cups to avoid hard labor and get into a hospital, said prison officers on August 5.

"It's a recent fashion: the first case

TRAVEL MISHAPS

❧ Two determined ambulancemen went to the wrong address, slapped a healthy Norwegian on a stretcher and rushed him to a hospital in Kragero, 40 miles away, despite his objections. Meanwhile, the real patient (who bore the same name and lived in the same village), suffering from severe anemia, drove himself to the hospital, where he struggled to register because a clerk insisted he was already there.

❧ Accused of hijacking an Olympic Airways jet, Kostas Tsenekides, 24, was released on bail when he explained that he was in a panic after swallowing a crucifix on take-off. When the pilot refused to believe it had lodged in his throat, the choking youth threatened to blow up the plane unless it made an emergency landing.

❧ Last July, a 32-year-old woman from the wardrobe department at Universal Studios in Hollywood got lost while driving on the lot and found herself following a tram. The tram proceeded down the middle of the "Red Sea" attraction, in which the waters are mechanically "parted." As soon as the tram completes the trip, the water is released, and the woman was thus trapped in the middle of the "sea" for about an hour until firemen rescued her.

bedded. They only choose the rusty ones and they put excrement on them."

Thirteen inmates in the Galati jail had nails in their heads. The shorter nails were just pulled out, while those going into the brain needed surgery. There are 45,000 convicts in Romania. Most jails are severely overcrowded and unhygienic.

....

TUMMY RUMBLES

....

An expert in *qi gong* breathing exercises demonstrates the alleged ability of her stomach to talk. Reporters in Langfang in China's Hebei province gather to record the abdominal words of wisdom, but as yet we have no information on what they were—or, indeed, if they could be understood.

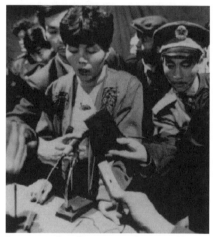

An expert in breathing exercises has trained her stomach to say more than, "I'm hungry."

....

STUMP FEVER

....

came to me in March," said Dr. Florin Vesa, head of the Galati county hospital in eastern Romania. "Today I operated on my seventeenth case. He is 23 years old and it was difficult to take the nail out. It was rusty and completely em-

For as long as he can remember, 68-year-old George Boyer admired and sought out the company of people who had limbs removed. More than anything else, he wanted to be an amputee himself. "No therapy has ever helped me with this overwhelming and irrational wish," he admitted in a TV documentary called "The Wannabees" in BBC2's "Over the Edge" series (July 12, 1994). So, for the last 18 years George planned to help himself. He experimented by shooting shoulders of pork and when he thought he had the distance and angle right he shot off his left leg.

"Immediately afterwards, I applied a tourniquet and tried to phone for help," but his bloody fingers kept slipping off the keypad. By the time help came "shock was setting in" and he became angry at the efforts to save his leg. "It took 12 days before they finally agreed to remove the limb," said George, who lives in Florida.

The same program featured a British man, identified only as Paul, who had also run a gauntlet of psychiatrists while seeking a surgeon to remove his healthy left leg. "It is a specific thing; it's about a body image," said Paul, who has tried damaging the unwanted limb by tourniquet, crushing and burning.

Psychologist Bryan Tully described the urge as a type of "stump fetishism" linked to a syndrome called dysmorphobia, a dislike of one's own body image also shared by anorexics and some people suffering from gender confusion. "They aspire to an idealized shape," he commented. "It can start with chopping off fingers and end by chopping off one bit after another. They are not mad. They can be well-organized, successful, creative people. It's just that they have this compulsion." Referring to a sub-genre of pornography involving amputees, Dr.

LOVE HURTS

❤ A naked couple's treetop lovemaking came to a climax when the woman plunged from the branches and broke her leg. Elizabeth Hooper and Jeff Healey had crept into Windsor Great Park in England for an all-night romp, choosing the oak tree close to the cavalry training grounds for their morning bout on August 2, 1994. Jeff, 35, climbed down, dressed hastily and went for help. In the meantime Elizabeth—a 29-year-old barmaid and ex-strippergram—was found, stark naked and in agony, by Crown Estates ranger Alastair Chamberlain. "It is a clear case of coitus interruptus," he said. Ms. Hooper was taken to Wexham Park Hospital in Slough. She was discharged after she was caught having sex in a busy ward with an unnamed man.

❤ Robert Hammontree, 29, and ex-wife Robyn Taylor, 41, from Corona del Mar, California, made naked love on a cliff top high on drink and drugs and tumbled to their deaths on rocks 100 feet below. Robert was the third of Robyn's four husbands—they had divorced in 1992.

❤ Christian Schneider, 24, was belting down a road at 70 miles per hour near Bersenbrueck, Germany, with his 15-year-old girlfriend Jenny riding him wearing only a bra. At the height of their passion, his car veered into an oncoming Audi, killing everyone involved.

❤ Jack Russell and Yorkshire terriers plunged over 100 feet down a cliff while mating in Tyne and Wear, England but recovered.

CULTURAL CURIOSITIES

❤ People convicted of crimes carrying the death sentence should be made to wrestle poisonous snakes inside a giant aquarium open to the public, according to Manila's "hanging judge," Maximiano Asuncion.

❤ Pakistani stockbrokers, in despair at a run that sent the Karachi Stock Exchange tumbling, sacrificed 10 goats in the parking lot to try and halt the crash. Turnover rose to a record 23.3 million shares, but the 100-share index fell again. The meat was given to the poor.

❤ The Afrikaans equivalent of "raining cats and dogs" is *reent oumeide met knopkieries* (raining grandmothers with knobkerries), while the Welsh equivalent is *bwrw hen wragedd a ffyn* (raining old women and sticks). What might this curious parallel signify?

❤ On Armistice Day (November 11), 1993, Australian radio announced the death of the Queen Mother. On Armistice Day, 1994, BBC TV's Ceefax made the same mistake. A line from the obituary rehearsal script was flashed on screen for almost a minute shortly after 11:30 A.M.

❤ Shop security alarms are being set off by Japanese love balls, the rubber-encased metal spheres worn internally for continuous stimulation, which have become a big fad with women executives. "I nearly died when I was grabbed and searched," said one 26-year-old graphic designer.

Tully added: "Stump fetishism is also associated with sexual fantasies."

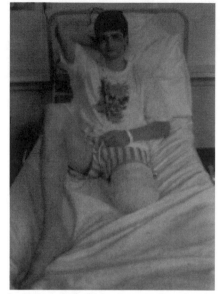

Ian Hudson, who lay his leg across a train track and fell asleep, is among the self-amputation enthusiasts.

There is no doubt in Paul's mind that he must lose part of himself to feel whole. "I am uncomfortable the way I am. The feeling is so deep-rooted, it will never go away." If he cannot find a surgeon-accomplice he will probably take the same drastic action that George did. The horror over, George now says he feels "free" for the first time in his life.

Terry Mills was legless in all senses of the word. A train took off his left leg just below the knee as he lay beside the track in Littleville, Alabama. It almost duplicated the accident eight years earlier in which he was deprived of his right leg in a similar fashion. On both occasions Mills was in a drunken stupor.

OUT WITH A BANG

Brian Kelly worked for a fireworks company in Osseo, Michigan, for six years. As he lay dying of complications from intestinal surgery, he told his family what to do with his ashes. According to his sister: "He got this big smirky smile on his face and said, 'I just want to be a big firecracker.' " On August 12, 1994, Kelly's ashes exploded from a 12-inch shell at a display during a convention of fireworks technicians.

SWEET SMELL OF SELF-IMMOLATION

Three copies of a $50 limited edition of Poppy Z. Brite's horror novel *Drawing Blood* were marked up to $600 in September 1994 because they smelled of burned human flesh. Two sold in less than a week after the plastic-wrapped books were advertised in the catalogue of Los Angeles rare book dealer Barry Levin.

On December 24, 1993, a man walked into Westwood Mail Services with a can of gasoline and set himself and the building on fire. He died a few days later, his motive unknown. The fire gutted the lobby of the delivery business, but most of the mail awaiting delivery, including a book shipment for Levin, was undamaged, except for a sickly-sweet odor. Levin gave the special edition profits to Westwood Mail Services to ease the cost of the fire.

SONS OF BITCHES: BOYS RAISED BY DOGS

ABANDONED BY PARENTS,
A NUMBER OF BOYS HAVE TURNED
TO FOSTER CANINES

👽 Berci Kutrovics, four, was discovered last November being reared by his family's two pet dogs in the village of Szil in western Hungary. He lived with the dogs in an outside shed. His single mother worked long hours and often left the boy alone. Staff at the Gyor

County children's home where he was taken found that he walked on all fours, growled, sniffed at his food before lapping it up and slept curled up in a corner. He could not talk, but responded to simple commands. Mihaly Szecsenyi, director of the children's home, said that the boy had learned to walk and use a spoon in the three weeks he had been in his care.

👽 An abandoned nine-year-old boy in a Romanian orphanage was suckled by a dog, the Rompres news agency reported last July. The child yelped and shared his food with the bitch who had raised him. "He kisses her with great affection and shares his canteen food with her," said the report. He was seven when he was put in the orphanage near Pitesti, 65 miles west of Bucharest, after living on the streets. He had not learned to speak. The other children called him "Moldin" after the bitch Molda which accompanied him.

👽 Horst-Werner Reinhart, age three, was brought up by an Alsatian named Asta in Mettmann, near Düsseldorf, while his parents spent days on end drinking in local bars. Asta scavenged for scraps to feed the boy and licked him clean. Police found them sharing a raw chicken. The only word he knew was "Asta." He whimpered like a dog and slept on the floor in a canine position, his head between his outstretched arms.

SCHWASCAR

THE SCHWASCAR AWARDS

STRANGE DEATH

❣ Slapstick comedian Yves Abouchar, 45, choked to death on a custard pie thrown in his face. The French star breathed in just as the pie landed and was suffocated by the foam.

RUNNERS-UP:

❣ Chef Juan Ruiz was stabbed through the heart with uncooked spaghetti strands when 150 mph winds hit his restaurant in Mexico City.

❣ Karate brown belt and Thai boxing enthusiast Scott Kell, 23, lost his balance doing high kicks and plunged to his death through an open window on the 10th floor of a tower block in Salford, England, on July 6, 1994.

❣ A young employee of the Bennett Food Factory in the Bronx, New York, died instantly when he fell headfirst into an industrial dough mixer making macaroni and was impaled by the mixing blades.

❣ A gum-chewing motorist was killed after he blew a giant bubble which burst and stuck to his glasses, blinding him. Abner Kriller, of Albany, Australia, ran his car off the road and plunged down a hill.

❣ Cory Quinn, from Sydney, Australia, committed suicide by locking himself in his estranged wife Mary's freezer when she went on holiday. He left a note for the 280-pound woman which said: "Gorge on this, you fat pig!"

❣ To support her ample frame, Berbel Zumner, 23, had to wear a bra reinforced with metal wires. These conducted a bolt of lightning which killed her as she was walking through a park in Vienna.

❣ Janet Smith, 28, walked into a grocery store in Gresham, Oregon, on August 21, 1994, holding a knife to the throat of her Siamese cat, and sat down in an aisle. Told by police to drop the knife, she threatened to kill the cat. Suddenly, she jumped up and began walking towards the police, who sprayed her with pepper mace. She then raised the knife above her head and charged at the police, who shot her dead. The cat escaped and could not be found.

❣ Robert Puelo, 32, entered a 7-Eleven in St. Louis on October 10, 1994, and started shouting and cursing. When an employee threatened to call the police, Puelo grabbed a hot dog, stuffed it down his throat and left the store without paying. The police discovered him unconscious and turning purple outside the store. He choked to death soon afterwards.

A four-year-old boy was found living with 60 dogs in Muskogee, Oklahoma, on August 29, 1989. "He howled. He reared back on his haunches, tilted his head and looked up," said his foster parent Cheryl Shropshire. "He ran wildly through the house, crashing into walls, and most of the time he ran on all fours. If he wanted attention, he would rub his head on us and whimper." The boy's mother had abandoned him when he was six months old. His grandparents, Gene and Joyce White, had caged him next to the dogs for two years. They were charged with failing to care for a minor, and faced up to a year in prison.

A boy from Hull, England, was locked in a shed with his family's dogs for long periods. He was taken into care at the age of 10. When he felt threatened, he would bark or growl, and would walk around in a circle before sitting down. He had very limited speech and it was thought that he had never been to school. Even after four years of therapy, the boy had not completely recovered.

Last May, there were reports of a boy living with a dog in a kennel in northern Italy. This was either in Collalbrigo, Conegliano, or "near Venice" and the boy was either eight, six or three. He barked, howled and crawled on all fours. One report said that his parents put him in the care of Silca, a German Shepherd bitch, because they were working in the fields 17 hours a day.

CORPSE STOLEN IN DALLAS

Melinda Ann Lee, 20, was knocked down by a drunk driver in Dallas, Texas, last October, dying from her injuries on Wednesday December 7, 1994. She was buried in Restland Memorial Park that Friday. Wayland Leroy Lamb Jr. was charged with intoxicated manslaughter and jailed the following Tuesday, December 13. That same day, cemetery staff discovered that someone had dug out the grave, bored through a concrete tomb cover, cracked open the coffin, and stolen the corpse, which probably took most of the night. No one living nearby heard anything. It was believed to be the first grave robbery in Dallas County for 50 years. On the morning of December 16, a newspaper delivery man found Miss Lee's body by the side of a South Dallas road. The police wondered if the episode was evidence of black magic or an obsessed admirer, but were still without a grave robber.

CUSTOM COFFIN CASE

A bizarre crucifix-shaped coffin, dumped on waste ground behind Gorton Fire Station in Manchester, England, was noticed lying on top of rubbish by a man walking his dog in early April, and caused much puzzlement. An undertaker pointed out that it was too wide for cremation and would need two burial plots in a graveyard. Was it something to do with Easter? Or a ritual object of some obscure cult?

This cruciform-shaped coffin mystified Manchester, England.

After a photo of the coffin appeared in a local paper on April 14, the mystery was solved. It had been designed by a Manchester advertising agency to promote a business equipment company. A man had been photographed in it surrounded by a computer, phone and so forth—the message being that firms should bury outdated office equipment. The agency, which asked not to be identified, presumed the coffin had been stolen before it was properly disposed of.

WEDDING DRESS MYSTERY

For the fifth time in four years, immaculate wedding day outfits have been found hanging in trees in Birkenhead Park in Liverpool, England. A teenager walking her dog early on Sunday morning, April 2, came upon a white wedding dress with a high collar, pearl buttons and a lacy, low-fronted top, together with a blue bridesmaid's dress, on a tree near a pile of stones.

In August last year, two dresses were found in exactly the same spot. Less than two weeks before the latest find, two schoolgirls found a similar pair of dresses near the park's old conservatory site.

"I think it is the same person doing this," said park ranger Dave Cavanagh, "because the dresses are always left in similar places—and hanging in a similar fashion."

THE CAVEWOMAN OF CYPRUS

A middle-aged woman with pigtails was discovered dying of starvation on April 6 in a 6-foot by 4-foot candlelit cave on the rugged Akamas peninsula near Paphos, on Cyprus's northwestern coast. She refused to speak or give any clue to her identity or nationality— although she communicated with hospital staff in Limassol by writing notes in English.

The woman had a flower tattooed on her stomach and by late May was claiming to be Maoysata, a Romanian gypsy who had run away from home at

LEGAL LUNACY

❦ Convicted murderer Allan Kinsella, 53, appearing in court charged with escaping from prison, sued the medium-security Canadian jail called the Bath Institution for aiding and abetting his escape on October 19. A ladder left behind by a builder was used to scale a fence.

❦ Ian Ord, 18, from County Durham, England, was remanded in custody for a retrial on a charge of stealing a car because he couldn't stop laughing at Teesside Crown Court. His lawyer said that he suffered from a "nervous disorder."

❦ Preacher Arthur Cornwall sued surgeons in South Africa for "extracting his soul" during a heart operation. He claimed to have lost his enthusiasm for Christianity.

❦ A Norwegian motorist, pulled over for a routine check near Bergen, called the policeman an "onion." For this he was fined $600. It was not clear whether other vegetable names would be considered equally insulting.

the age of 12, lived as a beggar and pavement artist all over Europe, until in Germany she fell in love with a United States serviceman called Joseph Eilats, who jilted her after a five-year affair. At other times, she claimed to be called Helen, Sophia or Mauguchata, a Polish Jew or a stowaway from Italy after all her belongings had been stolen.

The police believed none of it. They speculated she might have some connection to the headless, armless body of a middle-aged white man, found on the beach near the cave on May 20. Doctors thought her condition might have been caused by witnessing some horrific event.

What is now known is that she arrived in Cyprus on or about March 12, probably by boat on the south coast. Two days later, she asked a Greek Cypriot couple in Kouklia, between Limassol and Paphos, about cheap lodgings. They sent her to an old woman who put her up for two nights. Then she was spotted in the marketplace of Polis, 40 miles away. From there she traveled 10 miles west to the Baths of Aphrodite and then walked three miles along a precipitous path to the cave, 50 yards from the sea, where she spent the following three weeks surviving on oranges and water.

She drew a self-portrait depicting herself as an angelic figure and declared her wish to join a convent—but only if she could have male visitors. On May 27 she was pronounced sane and was sent to a Greek orthodox convent, St. Nicholas of the Cats, near Limassol. She had not gone to become a nun, but to help tend the 200 wild cats in the sanctuary. The nuns, in turn, said they would teach her to paint icons.

The convent's feline community dates back to the fourth century, when St. Helena of the Cross brought ferocious cats from Egypt to rid the drought-stricken island of an infestation of large snakes.

In early June, the woman was identified as Marie-Louise Birgitta Heinriz, 47, a Stockholm mother of two, after her brother recognized her picture in a Swedish newspaper. However, quite why she starved herself in a Cypriot cave remained unexplained.

VAMPIRE WANNABE

Lydia Buchan gave herself the "vampire name" Carlotta and extended her canines.

Lydia Buchan, 26, a secretary at Bristol University in England, is obsessed by vampires. She suffers from an unidentified disease which causes extreme sensitivity to sunlight and skin problems —but tests for suspected porphyria proved negative. A fatigue specialist said she had "a reverse body clock." "Daylight exhausts me and damages my immune system," she told journalist Jerry Taylor. "It just runs me down and I pick up any bug that's going." She has not been able to go to work since last October.

Ms. Buchan dresses in black and

TWISTED DUDES

❦ When New York builder Peter Jonson, 37, was shot in the head by a "drug-crazed sniper," he feared that taking himself to the hospital would incur great expense because he did not have any medical insurance. So he walked the few blocks to his home and removed the bullet himself with a pair of pliers.

❦ Fed up with his Ford Sierra, Craig Lambert, 23, fired seven shotgun cartridges into the troublesome car in his driveway in Gloucester, England. He was granted bail after facing charges of criminal damage. A month later, Joseph Berolino, 37, walked into a sawmill in Red Bluff, California, and fired 20 shots at a woodworking machine that had severely injured him two years earlier. The machine's paint was chipped, but it was not badly damaged.

❦ A Finnish man was found to be living with 20 dead cats under his bed and nearly 30 other ailing cats in his flat. Authorities had to destroy the survivors because of their poor state. Psychiatrists declared the man sane.

wears blood-red lipstick. Her house in the Bristol suburb of Westbury-on-Trym is festooned with rubber vampire bats. She has several black cats, is saving up for a coffin to sleep in, and plans to exchange her car for a second-hand hearse. She has given herself the "vampire name" Carlotta and has to wear sunglasses to look at her computer screen because the brightness irritates her. She had her canine teeth extended a few years ago to look like vampire fangs and had them lengthened still more last summer at a cost of $375. "I haven't bitten myself, but at first I talked with a bit of a lisp," she said. "Sometimes I flash them at kids to give them a scare. I love my steak really rare and dripping with blood...I've asked my local supermarket if they will let me buy animal blood."

IDENTITY CRISIS

An obsessed teenager tried to take over the life of her best friend. Sarah Talby, 18, met Ms. Corrine Scott when they both attended the London School of Fashion. She changed her hair color to match Ms. Scott's, took to wearing contact lenses as she did, changed her style of clothes and began rehearsing the use of her name. The final straw came when she tried to steal Ms. Scott's husband, Gregory. Scott, of Hackney, east London, beat Talby with a baseball bat, cut off her hair, shaved her eyebrows, and forced her to walk through the streets in her underwear. Scott was given a nine-month jail sentence, suspended for two years.

CULTS AND CONSPIRACIES

POSTMAN PAT IS A DIGITAL GANGSTER

Postman Pat is having trouble entering Japan because of his links to organized crime. Pat has only three fingers and a thumb, just like the Yakuza. The Japanese gangsters have a little finger amputated to demonstrate their loyalty and strength of character. Scholastic Children's Books, the Postman's publishers, have been asked to give him another digit before the tales appear in Japan.

Postman Pat must grow a finger to enter Japan.

YOU CAN'T BE SIRIUS

According to the Canadian police, a planned voyage to the Dog Star Sirius was behind the deaths in October of 53 people in Quebec and Switzerland linked to the Order of the Solar Temple. Cult members thought they could depart for the "planet Sirius" only after passing through a fiery death and carrying out the ritual slaying of an infant identified as the Antichrist. (Sirius is of course not a planet, but a star, the brightest in our night sky with a luminosity 23 times that of our sun.)

Cult leaders Joseph di Mambro and Luc Jouret chose three-month-old Christopher Emmanuel Dutoit as their human sacrifice. A wooden stake was driven through his heart in a Morin Heights chalet near Quebec. The infant's parents, Antonio Dutoit and Nicky Robinson, were stabbed to death and the chalet put to the torch.

PORK-POISONED AMMO

Chemist and Rabbi Moshe Antelman has invented a kind of bullet that will do more than kill Islamic terrorists physically. Contained within the bullets are small amounts of pork. Many Muslims believe that any contact with swine will kill their souls.

KURT COBAIN'S SUICIDE MACHINE

According to a press release by the Seattle-based cult "Friends Understanding Kurt" (FUK), the deaths of Nirvana singer Kurt Cobain and Hole bassist Kristin Pfaff were suicides linked to the use of "Dream Machines," the trance-inducing devices invented by William Burroughs collaborator Brion Gysin.

Nirvana? Kurt, Courtney and the babe before the "Dream Machine" nightmare.

The machines are basically cylinders with a light source inside that rotates, causing a flash 10.56 times per second, which induces a trance-like state. Various suicides were blamed on them in the 1960s when they first appeared.

Cobain is said to have learned of the machines while working with Burroughs. He obtained one from David Woodward in San Francisco, who made them to Gysin's specification. FUK claims that the rock star was using the machine for up to 72 hours at a time. It was found 20 feet from his body, but neither the police nor the coroner's office realized its significance.

Kristin Pfaff then obtained it and began using it on herself, against the wishes of Hole singer Courtney Love. Pfaff eventually killed herself with a heroin overdose. Spokespeople on all sides deny any knowledge of FUK, one describing it as a sick hoax, another as "Elvis sighted in 7-Eleven again."

WORLDWIDE WEIRDNESS

❦ The winners of the second annual beauty contest for Syrian goats, held near Riyadh in Saudi Arabia, were Miz'al and Wardi. Prizes included a car, gold pieces and $41,100.

❦ The Catholic Church in Austria has officially banned a 500-year-old anti-Semitic cult, popular in that region. The cult adores a small boy—Anderle, of the mountain village of Rinn—believed to have been ritually killed by Jews in the Middle Ages.

❦ North Korea reported further wonders following Kim Il-Sung's death. Cranes, swallows and bitterns were observed mourning and "twittering sadly." On the two-month anniversary of the Great Leader's passing, his favorite flower, the magnolia, had a miraculous late summer blooming. Popular grief was the bitterest experienced for 5,000 years.

❦ Russia's central command of the Strategic Rocket Forces, at Odintsovo outside Moscow, had its electricity supply cut off for 90 minutes on September 21 because it hadn't paid its bills, amounting to $6.75 million.

❦ The Islamic Salvation Army in Algeria has kidnapped Brahim Taouchichet, 45, the founding editor of the astrological magazine *Horoscope-Mysteres*. An "Islamic tribunal" was set to try him for unspecified crimes. Islam forbids astrology, as only God can predict the future.

DEATHS AND SUICIDES

POET JUDGED A POOR COVER

Oregon poet Dola Eugene Russell, who died on February 3, 1994, at the age of 62, did not after all get his last wish: to be skinned so that his hide could be used for binding a volume of his poetry. On April 4 his widow, Rachel Barton-Russell, settled a lawsuit brought by the state and agreed to have him cremated.

PICKLED STIFF GETS EARTHED

Henry Atkins was a worker at the Dixon Tobacco Company in Peducah, Kentucky—and a good friend of undertaker A. Z. Hamock. He was called "Speedy" because he was a fast worker. On May 30, 1928, he was fishing from the bank of the Tennessee River near Owens Island when, drunk on hooch, he fell in

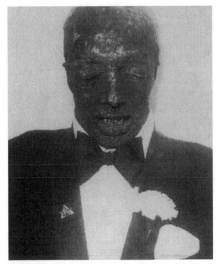

Speedy has enjoyed the benefits of homemade embalming fluid since 1928.

and drowned. He was in his fifties.

As Speedy had no family, Hamock used him to demonstrate his home-made embalming fluid. The body turned the color of rust, with yellowed teeth visible through retracted lips. Hamock took the secret of his embalming fluid to the grave in 1948, while Speedy continued to hang around in his tuxedo, mostly in a cupboard at the Hamock Funeral Home. He was washed and dressed three times a year to keep mold off. In the summer, Hamock's widow, Velma, would take Speedy out of the cupboard for sightseers, free of charge. Finally, she thought that 66 years of waiting was long enough, and she arranged for Speedy's interment. On August 5, 200 people bade him farewell with spirituals and sermons at the Washington Street Baptist Church in Paducah and he was lowered into a grave at Maplelawn Cemetery.

SPEEDY IS NOT THE
ONLY PICKLED STIFF:

The preserved body of Buddhist monk Pu Chao, who died 11 years ago in a southern Taiwan cave, is attracting thousands of pilgrims. Visitors can see the body in the cave behind Kungcheng Temple in Shenshui village. They may even shake his hand.

Pu Chao died at age 93 while meditating in the cave in January 1983. He told his disciples in their dreams not to move his body, which was robed and reclining in a seat. Ever since, the disciples have cleaned the corpse once a week using a piece of wet cloth. The body gives off no smell and the muscles are elastic. His body hair has even been growing, the disciples say. They believe Pu Chao achieved "golden-body" status because of his high virtues and rigid Buddhist lifestyle—he lived on a

LOST AND FOUND

☥ Postman Bill O'Reilly managed to deliver a letter addressed to "Gwen and Norman—somewhere near Wadebridge, England" after he saw a photo of the couple in the "window" of the envelope. He recalled that the woman was a customer at a Cornwall grocery where he had worked as a boy some 30 years earlier.

☥ Hector Paez was too poor to afford a cataract operation to save his sight, so he stole two eyeballs from a hospital in Argentina. He was arrested while begging a surgeon to swap them for his own defective orbs.

☥ After years of searching, botanists in New Zealand found an orchid thought extinct. It was lying flattened under a ground sheet when they took down their tent.

☥ Notice seen in a Swiss mountain inn: "Special today—no ice cream."

diet of tree leaves and rainwater. The incorrupt bodies of two other Buddhist monks—Tru Hang (died 1954) and Ching Yen (died 1970)—have been preserved in earthen jars.

Meanwhile on the Taiwan mainland, the body of an 88-year-old woman who died in Xianghe county, Hubei province, had not stiffened or decomposed eight months after her death. The life-long vegetarian had asked for her body not to be cremated or interred. Chinese scientists launched an investigation.

REQUIEM FOR DR. LOBOTOMY

November saw the passing of James Watts, the American neurosurgeon who, with Walter Freeman, popularized the pre-frontal lobotomy as a cure for all human sadness and a tool for social control. Between 1936 and the early 1960s, they performed at least 700 lobotomies. Watts pushed a steel probe right through the front of the subject's brain under local anaesthetic. This was often done before an audience, with

Freeman urging the patient to sing "God Bless America" or "Mary had a Little Lamb." Freeman once asked a patient: "What's going through your mind now?" To which came the reply: "A knife."

Both lobotomizers seem to have been mildly unhinged themselves. Freeman attempted to prove that Freudian analysts were suicidal depressives, presumably ripe for skewering; at one point he had a nervous breakdown which, according to Watts's obituary in the *Daily Telegraph*, "left him with a lasting animosity towards the brain."

FREE-FALL FOUL-UP

At the 1994 annual awards dinner given by the American Association for Forensic Science, AAFS President Don Harper Mills astounded his audience in San Diego with the legal complications of a bizarre death. Here is the story:

"On March 23, 1994, the medical examiner viewed the body of Ronald Opus and concluded that he died from a shotgun wound of the head. The decedent had jumped from the top of a ten-story building intending to commit suicide (he left a note indicating his despondency). As he fell past the ninth floor, his life was interrupted by a shotgun blast through a window, which killed him instantly. Neither the shooter nor the decedent was aware that a safety net had been erected at the eighth floor level to protect some window washers and that Opus would not have been able to complete his suicide anyway because of this."

"Ordinarily," Dr. Mills continued, "a person who sets out to commit suicide ultimately succeeds, even though the mechanism might not be what he intended. That Opus was shot on the way to certain death nine stories below probably would not have changed his mode of death from suicide to homicide. But the fact that his suicidal intent would not have been successful caused the medical examiner to feel that he had homicide on his hands.

"The room on the ninth floor whence the shotgun blast emanated was occupied by an elderly man and his wife. They were arguing and he was threatening her with the shotgun. He was so upset that, when he pulled the trigger, he completely missed his wife and the pellets went through the window striking Opus.

"When one intends to kill subject A but kills subject B in the attempt, one is guilty of the murder of subject B. When confronted with this charge, the old man and his wife were both adamant that neither knew that the shotgun was loaded. The old man said it was his long-standing habit to threaten his wife with the unloaded shotgun. He had no intention to murder her—therefore, the killing of Opus appeared to be an accident. That is, the gun had been accidentally loaded.

"The continuing investigation turned up a witness who saw the old couple's son loading the shotgun approximately six weeks prior to the fatal incident. It transpired that the old lady had cut off her son's financial support and the son, knowing the propensity of his father to use the shotgun threateningly, loaded the gun with the expectation that his father would shoot his mother. The case now becomes one of murder on the part of the son for the death of Ronald Opus."

There was an exquisite twist. "Further investigation revealed that the son [who, it turns out, *was* Ronald Opus] had become increasingly despondent over the failure of his attempt to engineer his mother's murder. This led him to jump off the ten-story building on March 23, only to be killed by a shotgun blast through a ninth story window.

"The medical examiner closed the case as a suicide."

The source for this story is obscure. Several correspondents forwarded it from various odd Usenet groups.

....

FREEZE-FRAMED

....

Ted Flynn, 48, arrived at his daughter's third-floor flat in Stechford, England, at midnight on December 22, 1994, and found she was out, so he tried to get in from a balcony via the bathroom window. Tragically, he got stuck halfway through and froze to death as temperatures fell to −7°C. His legs were spotted by a postman delivering mail the following morning.

A man stuck in his daughter's window froze solid.

MANIAC SURGEON

At the beginning of July 1994, the remains of Berlin prostitute Dana F., 23, were recovered from the River Havel near Oranienburg, Germany, neatly cut into 40 pieces. Then, on November 5, the head of another young woman was found in a dustbin at a service area off the A1 autobahn near Lübeck. The woman's heart, lungs and kidneys were found at the next service area. The heads of both victims had been cut off flush with the skull, leaving no evidence of strangulation. The precision of all the cuts convinced the police that a portable laser scalpel had been used.

WHAT'S IN A NAME?

❦ Magistrate Kathleen Crook was charged in February 1994 with submitting false claims for loss of earnings and expenses while sitting on the bench at Bournemouth—though she insisted she was innocent. By contrast, Frances Crook, director of the Howard League for Penal Reform, is a paragon of virtue.

❦ John Hustler, former head of venture capital at KPMG Peat Marwick, teamed up with Quester Capital Management, a specialist investment boutique, to create a "dating" agency, matching private investors with business ideas.

❦ The family of a Greek farmer were grief-stricken when they heard he had died in a motorcycle accident. But Lazarus Agriodimos rose from the dead: during his wake he walked in announcing that he had lent his bike to a friend.

❦ Fleetus Lee Gobble, 45, choked to death on food in the K&W Cafeteria in Winston-Salem, North Carolina.

❦ Neil and Teresa Tantrum, from Rhondda, England, went to Tonyrefail Comprehensive after their 15-year-old daughter complained that other children were bullying her. Mrs. Tantrum yanked hair from one girl's head and chipped her tooth. Mr. Tantrum yelled obscenities. Both admitted "affray" at Cardiff Crown Court and were sent to jail for four months.

❦ Sarah Careless, 26, from Tamworth, near Birmingham, was given a brand-new Peugeot 306 Cabriolet as an anniversary present. She was involved in a head-on crash within minutes of setting off on her first journey. She escaped injury, but the repair bill was over $3,000.

❦ A Greek Cypriot woman was hit on the head and knocked out when an icon fell on her in church. The wound required nine stitches. Nina Theophanous said later that the episode was "divine intervention" and that she was convinced that God had sent her a message. The woman's surname means "God manifests."

GENIUS AND DISCOVERY

AND ROBOT BEGOT ROBOT

Yoshiaki Ichikawa's team at the Hitachi Energy Research Laboratory in Tsukuba, 50 miles north of Tokyo, has invented a self-reproducing automaton, using microchips as "genetic codes." The centipede-like metal creature assembles itself from 8x4x4-inch block components to "grow" to twice its original size before splitting into two identical and independent units. Ichikawa predicted that the genetic codes could soon be programmed to create random "mutants." The mutant best adapted to its work environment would produce more offspring, thus embodying the Darwinian hypothesis of natural selection.

HASN'T LEARNED ABOUT ROUNDING UP

Zhang Zhuo, 12, from China's Sichuan province, recited the value of pi to the 4,000th place in 25 minutes and 30 seconds at a demonstration attended by psychologists, officials and reporters. The error rate was 0.2 percent.

SEVERED SOUVENIRS: ELVIS'S WART AND EINSTEIN'S BRAIN

Galileo's finger bone resides in an ornate reliquary in the Medici Collection of Scientific Instruments in Florence. Byron's lungs are kept in a jar somewhere in Greece. Elvis's wart and a bit of gristle purporting to be Napoleon's penis have both graced auction houses in recent years; and Oliver Cromwell's preserved head spent centuries being passed from owner to owner until its final burial a few years back. Albert Einstein, however, is not someone you would associate with this motley parade of anatomical Flying Dutchmen—until now.

Einstein's eyeballs were discovered in a New Jersey bank vault.

When Einstein died in April 1955, he was cremated and his ashes scattered at a secret location (probably the Delaware River) in order to avoid creating a "shrine" for admirers.

The first sign of Einstein's claim to a place in the spare parts pantheon was transmitted to the world on All Fool's Day 1994, when the Arena "Relics" series broadcast a wholly unbelievable documentary about a Japanese professor's search for Einstein's brain. The date, the entirely surreal progress of the search and the appearance of William Burroughs as a TV repair man, all contributed to the aura of "hoax."

Only it wasn't a hoax; the search was real, the prof was real and the date "purely coincidental." Einstein's brain—well, several large sections of it—really is stored in three jars under the sink in the tiny apartment of Dr. Thomas Harvey in Lawrence, Kansas. Harvey had already given pieces to Dr. Schulman of Chicago for Christmas, and to a Dr. Boyd who still has it in his fridge labeled "Big Al's Brain." In the documentary, yet another fragment was presented to the deeply bowing Japanese professor.

As it transpired, the trail of bits and pieces did not end there, for a few months later news came that Einstein's eyeballs were found in a jar in a New Jersey bank vault, the property of the great man's optician Dr. Henry Abrams. Given that Einstein was cremated within two days of dying, how did these organs go for a walk?

The answer lies in the autopsy room. Far from the dispassionate medical investigation one imagines, Einstein's autopsy was a body snatcher's free-for-all. Harvey, the hospital's resident pathologist, scooped out the physicist's brain and pickled it on the spot, intending to do a detailed study of it to reveal the source of Einstein's genius. The research was never done and Harvey, now 82, is working in a plastics factory, having lost his medical license.

Abrams, with the permission of the hospital administrator, spent 20 minutes disconnecting Einstein's eyeballs, apparently with no other intention than keeping them as a memento. The looting may not have stopped there—apparently, Einstein's heart and intestines were observed the next day in a bucket.

It makes one think about other famous stiffs. In *Goddess*, Anthony Summer's biography of Marilyn Monroe, the author mentions that her makeup artist had to fabricate artificial breasts when preparing her for burial, the real ones having been "destroyed" during the autopsy. In the light of Einstein's fate, this takes on a more macabre aspect. What will turn up next?

TWISTED DUDES

❤ When 14-year-old Alex Geveart was rushed to the hospital after a crash in Lisbon, Portugal, doctors heard ticking from his stomach through their stethoscopes. Alex explained: "Two years ago I swallowed my watch for a bet. It's still there."

❤ Five prison guards in Boise, Idaho, were moved after they taunted death row inmates by piping in Neil Young's 1971 song "The Needle and the Damage Done" on the night murderer Keith Wells died by lethal injection.

❤ A man gnawed the skin off all his fingertips in Binghamton, New York, after being arrested in connection with drugs and firearms offenses. Police had to wait for the skin to grow back before he could be fingerprinted.

SO THAT'S WHAT THEY DO BETWEEN CUSTOMERS

Indian bank teller Om Prakesh Singh has entered the record books after threading a needle 20,675 times in two hours. Singh already holds a national record for squeezing 61,800 letters onto a birthday greetings postcard.

HOAXES AND PANICS

HEAD CASES

Modern caricatures mistaken for Celtic Stonecraft.

These heads, unearthed in the 1960s in a garden in Fence, England, were until recently displayed in the Pendle Heritage Centre as examples of Celtic stonecraft. They are, in fact, caricatures of Hitler and Mussolini, carved by architect's apprentice Leslie Ridings in 1939, which often went on show during war-time dances. Ridings was killed on D-Day while trying to land a glider in France. His brother Ted, from Brierfield, said: "The heads ended up at our mother's house and when I sold the place to the late Mr. Roger Preston in 1966 I was so busy that I forgot to clear it out properly. I forgot all about the heads until I found them in a local history book."

THAT AIN'T NO LADY

A missing person report filed by Bruce Jensen in Bountiful, Utah, last April led to the unmasking of his "wife" as a man called Felix Urioste who had defrauded Jensen of $40,000–$60,000 during their marriage of three and a half years.

The deception unraveled in May when Urioste, 34, was pulled over for speeding in Nevada and police found 33 credit cards and other identification in 19 different names, as well as keys to four hospitals in Salt Lake City. At the time, he was traveling as a man with an 18-year-old male companion. Police later established that he had enrolled as a female student at the University of Utah and had worked as a doctor in the four Salt Lake hospitals, alternating between male and female aliases.

Jensen, 39, was a lab technician at University Hospital, Salt Lake City, in September 1991 when he met Urioste, or "Leasa Bibianna Herrera," a female doctor with a "Cleopatra-style" wig and heavy makeup. According to Urioste's family, he had run away from home at 13 and told them at 17 that he had a sex-change operation, after which they referred to him as a female.

THE UNIVERSITY OF UTAH

Signature

LEASA BIBIANNA HERRERA
U585-51-2695

UNDERGRADUATE STUDENT

Felix Urioste, dressed as a woman, maintained a marriage with an unsuspecting man for three and a half years.

Urioste told Jensen that he was an Israeli disowned by his parents for marrying a non-Jew, and had later joined the Mormons. After a single sexual encounter, he said he was pregnant with twins and Jensen felt morally obliged to give the children a father. They were married in December 1991. Several months later, Urioste claimed to have cancer and said that the twins were stillborn. He was able to pull off the deception because Jensen never saw him naked and the marriage was essentially celibate.

The couple was married in the Mormon church and Jensen was widely

THE SCHWASCAR AWARDS

SCHWASCAR

FOOLISH FELON

🛸 Edilber Guimaraes, 19, was arrested in Belo Horizonte, Brazil, in November 1993 for attempted theft at a glue factory. He had stopped to sniff some of the glue he was stealing, keeled over and spilled two cans, sticking himself to the floor. He was found 36 hours later and had to be cut loose by firemen.

RUNNERS-UP:

🛸 Pierre Cologne dashed into a pawnshop in Nice, France, and told owner Claude Montand: "Wait there with your hands up. I'll be back with my gun." When he returned, the staff disarmed him.

🛸 Convincing forgeries of 50,000-ruble notes (worth about $33) turned up in Vologda, 240 miles north of Moscow, last September. The forgers had made one mistake, however: the word "Russia," appearing prominently on the top of the bill, had a letter missing. The police believed the counterfeit cash came from Chechnya.

🛸 A man walked into a pharmacy in Vernon, British Columbia, in early January and told an employee he was going to rob the place—but would be back in 30 minutes to do it. When he came back with a buddy, the police were waiting.

🛸 Robert Ventham, 22, took his golf clubs with him on a cannabis-buying trip to Gibraltar, with the idea of fooling Customs as to the purpose of his visit. As yet, there are no golf courses on the Rock. Ventham was arrested on his return for possession of two kilos of dope.

🛸 Six masked raiders ambushed an armored security van carrying $1.5 million at Crawley near Winchester, England, forced it off the road and burned a two-foot hole in the side with blowtorches. Thousands of bank notes were burnt to ashes while further bundles were left unusable, damaged by smoke and heat. In the confusion, the van driver drove off while a colleague raised the alarm. They had to stop after 200 yards as the cab filled with smoke. By then the robbers had fled empty-handed.

🛸 Raiders stole some 200 training shoes from a sports shop in Alfreton, England. They will be hard-pressed to find a ready market for them as they are all for left feet.

respected for the care he gave his "cancer-stricken" wife while working two jobs. Urioste fled the marriage in April, saying he was going to New York for cancer treatments. In reality, he had started wavering in his intention to complete sex-change surgery. He had had his testicles but not his penis removed and was taking female hormones that gave him slight breasts. He stopped taking the hormones in the spring; at the time of the arrest, he had a thick moustache.

After the imposture was exposed, Jensen sought an annulment, citing irreconcilable differences (not to mention similarities). Confused, embarrassed and broke, he planned to return to his native Wyoming and "crawl in a hole for a few years and not let anyone within rifle range."

THE GOBLIN OF CHEDDAR

"John," a 33-year-old radiographer from Bournemouth, England, returned from working in Saudi Arabia with a photo he believed to be the world's first distinct evidence of a race of cave-dwelling goblins.

The man—who for reasons that will become clear, wishes to remain pseudonymous—had overheard colleagues talking about the picture, taken in a nearby cave or chasm. The person who took the photograph told John that he had seen a flash of light among the rocks, snapped in the general direction with his camera and this weird figure turned up on a print when it was later devel-

CANNIBAL COURSES

❦ In a 12-page confession, Gretchen Steinfurt told German police how she killed and dismembered her husband Hermann, and then served him up to her boyfriend in ham hock soup. At her trial, Conrad Krueger, the unwitting cannibal, said: "I knew it didn't taste like any ham hocks I ever had before. It was rather gamey." Steinfurt was jailed for life.

❦ Twelve "devil worshippers" ordered take-out pizzas from the Buen Apetito pizza parlor in Buenos Aires. They were delivered to an abandoned factory in a run-down industrial area of the Argentine capital by Carlos Sanchez, aged 19. His employer reported him missing and police raided the factory. Nine fiends escaped, but three were found dressed in white gowns around a candlelit table. They had ignored the pizzas but had eaten the delivery boy. All that remained were his bones.

❦ Yuri Lukin, a doorman at the railway hospital in the central Russian town of Saratov, raided the hospital refrigerator on November 12, 1993, stole some body parts and sold them as cooking meat at a local market to raise money for drink. One woman said she bought some meat for the unusually low price of 1,200 rubles (then about $1.05) and rushed back to work to boast about her bargain buy. Her colleagues noticed surgical sutures binding together a wound, and human-looking hair. A plastered Lukin was soon arrested. He was sent to jail for two years in April 1994.

STRANGE DEATHS

❂ Glen Pelmear, 33, was electrocuted while sitting on a public lavatory at Ryde on the English Isle of Wight. A broken light fitting had made the whole row of all-metal cubicles "live." Police found the body on Saturday night, July 8, with sparks still showering from it. They initially announced that vandals had tampered with the wiring and if caught would be charged with manslaughter; later they said it was an accident.

❂ Debbie Menta, 32, and Doug Painter, 23, children of the San Diego Chargers quarterback coach Dwain Painter, stood on a high rock above the sea near Mendocino, California, on February 2, to scatter the ashes of their mother, who had committed suicide the previous month. They were swept into the sea by a powerful wave; Debbie was drowned while her brother struggled to safety.

❂ Hans Pendner, from Salzburg, Austria, suffocated when he became entangled in 60 feet of thick wallpaper and couldn't struggle free. "The more he struggled, the tighter the paper wrapped him up," said detective Peter Dieker.

❂ Elderly golfer Jean Potevan threw his golf bag into a lake after missing three putts on the final hole of a disastrous round at Orleans (or Lyons—the reports disagree) in France. Realizing that his car keys were in the bag, he waded in fully clothed and drowned when he got entangled in weeds as he dived under the water. According to fellow player Henri Levereau, his last words were: "I'm going back for the keys, but I'm leaving the clubs down there."

oped. Locals shown the photo said it was a *djinn* (an Islamic demon).

Before he returned home, John asked for a print. "As soon as I saw it I was fascinated," he told David Haith, columnist for the *Bournemouth Advertiser*.

Everyone who saw the goblin photo was curious and impressed. Thinking the picture might be worth something, he placed it in a bank and began to seek a buyer; he even approached *FT*.

In this case caution was the best strategy, for the *Bournemouth Advertiser's* publication of John's murky picture brought an unequivocal identification of the creature—it was a sculpture at the famous Cheddar Showcaves & Gorge in Somerset, England.

This sculpture was mistaken for evidence of a race of cave-dwelling goblins.

Bob Smart, manager of the attraction, said the goblin was a figure in their Crystal Quest exhibition which has attracted nearly one million visitors since it opened in March 1991. This man-made Fantasy Grotto features Tolkien-esque figures of dragons, goblins, dwarves, wraiths and a Lord of Darkness, occasionally lit at random in the gloom. Smart said they were often contacted by people who had taken flash photos in the darkness and been surprised to find fantastic creatures on their prints. There is a lesson here for all of us.

....

MUPORE MESSIAH

....

Janet Amongi, 37, six months pregnant, stunned her neighbors in the Lira district of Uganda on September 17, 1994, by announcing that an angel had told her in a dream that she would deliver a boy on December 5 who would redeem the world. He was to be called "Aciro Mupore" (holy sufferer). Ms. Amongi, who comes from the Chawente sub-county of Apac district, told the jeering and cursing crowd in Lira New Market extension square that she was not allowed to let an uncleansed person touch her belly. She was believed to be possessed.

ARCHIVE GEMS

THE ILLINOIS ENEMA BANDIT

The chronicles of crime feature few more desperate characters than Michael Kenyon, a petty criminal who forcibly administered enemas to at least two dozen victims, mostly female students, between 1965 and 1975. Face hidden behind a ski mask, he would break into a woman's room, tie her up and get to work with his rubber tubing. Part of his ritual was to steal a single item from each victim; then, leaving the student trussed and terrified, he would sometimes phone the police to boast about his crime.

The Enema Bandit first struck while studying at the University of Illinois. Kenyon committed a dozen assaults between 1965 and 1969 before graduating with a degree in accountancy. From college he joined the army, before taking to cleaning people out for a living as an employee of the Internal Revenue Service. As he was posted around the country, enema attacks occurred in Los Angeles, Manhattan, KS and Norman, OK. On one occasion he administered an enema to a girl in a train traveling to Florida.

By May 1974, the Bandit was back on home turf, attacking several University of Illinois coeds in a single night. The police made little headway in tracing the culprit until Kenyon was arrested in connection with two robberies near Champaign, Illinois, in April 1975. Someone noticed that the method of breaking and entering was identical to that of the Enema Bandit and Kenyon was charged with armed robbery and battery. He served six years in prison and was paroled in 1981.

Former FBI agent John Finley, who researched the case for *Fortean Times*, notes that Kenyon was a subscriber to *Enema Digest*, a specialist magazine for devotees of water sports. There is no record of further enema assaults since 1981.

INEPTITUDE AND STUPIDITY

KILLED WHILE SHOWING CHEEK

Hamish Nuttall, 20, walking home with fellow students after a party near Chelmsford, England, was killed by a car after he "mooned" drivers. The trial of driver Justin Cheek, 21, was dismissed for lack of evidence.

PURPOSEFUL PRIEST PUNCHER

Ettore Gagliano, 86, is in a psychiatric hospital after punching a priest in the Milan Duomo—his 158th clerical victim to date. "I'm quite sane. I have a mission in life," said Ettore, who likes to ambush his prey from under the cathedral eaves.

LITTLE DEVILS

When 30-year-old Shigeharu Sato wanted to name his son Akuma (meaning "demon') after a distinctive cartoon character, the municipal authority in Akishima, Japan, rejected his application and ordered him to rename the boy. Sato objected and instantly became a media celebrity, as much for making a fuss in public, one suspects, as for picking such an unusual name (most Oriental cultures frown on names which might attract bad luck or the attention of the gods). The abuse and limitation of the Japanese naming laws were hotly debated on the street and at Cabinet level.

So goes the account in Western papers, anyway. According to the Japanese daily *Yomiuri* (Feb. 16, 1994), the proud but obstinate father is actually called Ya-

suhiro Tanoka and he runs a snack shop in the Akishima suburb of Tokyo. Tanoka says his first choice—which translates as "Little Flower Plucked from Hairy Bottom"—came to him in a dream. As he tells it: "At first the official wrote it down but, after consulting with a superior, he came back, crossed it out and said that it was rude and if I didn't choose a name that conformed to social norms he'd call the police."

Faced with such petty bureaucracy, Tanoka took the matter to the Tokyo Family Court, which initially ruled in his favor. "They said I had abused my naming rights, but since the name had been written in the register it should not have been crossed out." The municipal officials stood firm, refusing to reinstate the name, so Tanoka, after considering Jin ("God"), offered to change it to Akuma, meaning "something else."

"I did not want to cause offense, but they threw me out of the building. I appealed again to the Family Court, but they said I had to call him something else. So that is what I'm going to call him."

A similar idiocy occurred in November 1993, when Clive Kirke, a vicar in Litherland, England, objected to baptizing Gaynor Brennan's son Damian because it was the demon's name in the *Omen* films.

TRULY, THE PITTS

Three members of a family, described as "Britain's worst neighbors," were jailed on September 16, 1994, for setting fire to their terraced house in Ashington, Northumberland, only two days after taking out contents and building insurance worth $150,000 in November 1992. John Pitt, 48, and his wife Mary, 47, got seven years, while son David, 20, got six years' youth custody.

Are the Pitts Britain's worst neighbors?

The family was seen loading furniture into a van and dumping plastic bags holding their belongings in the garden only hours before the house went up "like a bomb" with the help of gasoline. The parents and six of their eight children, along with five dogs, two cats, two bikes and a moped, then turned up at the home of Mary Pitt's brother, whom they had not seen for three years, as their house blazed only streets away. When the Pitts left town to live temporarily in a caravan, their neighbors threw a street party.

LETHAL LOYALTIES

William Powell, 35, was convicted of assault in Detroit for pulling his pregnant, 33-year-old girlfriend partway through the window of his van as he sped through the neighborhood, ramming her against a telephone pole and kicking her after he stopped the van. The woman, who lost the baby as well as an arm and a leg in the incident, testified in support of Powell, saying the incident was her fault.

STUBBORN BASTARD

Israel's most stubborn man, a Yemeni called Yahiya Avraham, died in jail on December 4, 1994, at age 81, a week after suffering a cerebral hemorrhage. For more than four decades, he had refused to say three simple words needed to divorce his wife—"I am willing."

Avraham married his wife, Ora, 66, in Yemen when she was 12 years old and he was 28. She bore him two daughters, but he berated her for not bearing sons. Twelve years later, the family was living in Israel, and Ora petitioned a rabbinical court for divorce. "His behavior was abhorrent," she told the newspaper *Yedioth Ahronoth*. "He treated me like a chattel."

According to Jewish law, both parties must agree to a divorce. Ever since 1950, rabbis have beseeched Avraham to say the three necessary words. He was thrown in jail in 1962, having persistently vowed never to agree; he remained there for the rest of his life. Delegations visited him there over the years, trying to persuade him to change his mind. In February 1993, for instance, he withstood pleas from seven rabbis for two hours. They offered him freedom, a fancy apartment and religious blessings. One sang melancholy Yemeni songs to try and soften the man's heart. All he would say was: "Can't do it, can't do it, go away."

PECULIAR PRESS

MAN LIVED IN HOLE AFTER FAKING DEATH AT SEA
Daily Telegraph,
May 28, 1994

MOUSE STARTED FIRE AT STADIUM
Bristol Evening Post,
June 4, 1994

MAYENDE LOVES HIS 4 LEGGED COCK
The Monitor (Uganda),
June 7, 1994

"He's destroyed my life; may his name be destroyed," his wife told *Yedioth* in 1993. "I haven't seen his ugly puss since 1967 and I hope never to see him again."

Recalcitrant husbands are hardly ever jailed, and even then only for short periods. "To our knowledge there has never been a case even resembling this one," said prison spokesman Dubi Ben-Ami.

NUT CASES

❤ The courtroom in Manassas, Virginia, that staged the Bobbitt drama in 1994 heard another odd case on February 15, 1995. Edward G. Kelly, 44, of nearby Falls Church, was charged with raping a woman of 26 he met several months earlier when they were in group therapy. Both Kelly and the victim claim to suffer from multiple-personality disorder (MPD). Kelly was accused of tying up the woman with wire and raping her on May 18, 1994, in her home in a Washington suburb. His defense was that one of his personalities, "Spirit," and one of hers, "Laura," consented to sex. "There was no forcing…there was no hurting anybody," Kelly said in court papers. "Spirit loved Laura."

❤ Another trial involving alleged MPD started in Hamilton County, Ohio, in October 1994. Bus driver Joseph Howard was accused of raping a 22-year-old woman, allegedly with ten personalities, on June 16. According to Howard, two of her alter egos consented to sex.

❤ Not all psychiatrists—or judges—accept the existence of MPD. Manhattan Supreme Court Judge Leslie Snyder, for instance, rejected career criminal Hubert Napier's defense of MPD as "unadulterated crap" as she jailed him for the rest of his life. Napier, 27, who decapitated and gutted Kim Nichols in her New York apartment in 1990 and went on a spending spree with her credit cards, claimed the atrocity was ordered by a god called Zygor, a voice called George and a dog called Demolition who shared his mind with four other personalities.

❤ A French lawyer suffering from MPD created a legal tangle by trying to sue his six alter egos. "They have ruined my life," said Jean-Luc Pollard. A judge had to decide whether to allow the case of *Pollard v Pollard, Pollard, Pollard, Pollard, Pollard and Pollard.*

THE
ANIMAL
WORLD

THE ANIMAL WORLD

Anything that animals do or have done to them is included here. Out-of-Place Animals, for example, are animals that turn up where they shouldn't—like alligators in the sewers of New York or penguins off the coast of Italy. Manimals include the likes of bigfoot, Yeti, and the Chinese wild man. Water Monsters, which were a dime a dozen this year, include the Loch Ness Monster and its cousins around the world.

Weirdness red in tooth and claw was slightly up in 1995. New Species received a boost when an entire new phylum was discovered—a creature which lives on lobsters' lips. Overall it was a wonderfully weird year in the animal kingdom.

OUT-OF-PLACE ANIMALS

LET YOUR FINGERS FIND THE FALCON

Harry Walker, 69, of Belper, England, tried to phone the police to see if there was any news of his pet falcon, Lenny, which had disappeared the day before, on February 7. He misdialed and spoke to a family in Wyver Lane, several streets away, who told him that the bird was perched on their fence.

CAMEL CLEAN

Lita Nahas, 46, has gone into business with her window-washing camels. "I just mix sugar with the soap," she explained to the Cairo press. "I put it on the windows and the camels lick it off. We can do an entire ground floor in minutes."

GOLFER HOOKS MONSTER PIKE

After hooking his ball, golfer Lennie Learmouth searched a flooded bunker with a rake and landed a four-foot, 40-pound pike on the 12th hole at Wetherby Golf Club, West Yorkshire, England.

Mr. Learmouth, 62, believes the fish was bunkered when the River Wharfe burst its banks two weeks earlier. He was helped in his catch by his golf partner George Leafe, after which they put the pike back in the river. The bunker pond was only 18 inches deep. "The water exploded when we touched it. It was an ugly, vicious looking creature," said Mr. Learmouth, a retired insurance salesman from Boston Spa. A spokesman for *Angling Times* said: "A pike of that size is a real monster."

GATOR GAWKING

A 10-foot bull alligator took up residence in an apartment sewer pipe in North Miami Beach, Florida, in July 1993. It feasted on everything from chicken bits to chocolate bars and large crowds turned up to gawk at it through the sewer grate. A team of trappers led by Todd Hardwick had failed to corner the critter after three days.

SPIDERS COLONIZE HAMPSTEAD

London's Hampstead Heath has been host to some strange creatures over the centuries—the latest on eight legs. The rare tube-web spider, cousin of the bird-eating tarantula, has been discovered in a 100-strong colony in an isolated part of the heath, where it was last seen in 1892.

The colony only covers 10 square yards on a steep, grassy slope facing

PECULIAR PRESS

PSYCHOTIC WHITE RHINO BOARDS FREEDOM FLIGHT
Bangkok Post, Jan. 21, 1994

ANCIENT BLONDE CORPSES RAISE QUESTIONS
Times Herald Record (Poughkeepsie, NY), Mar. 18, 1994

ATTACK BY ET PROVES COSTLY
Brisbane Courier Mail, Mar. 18, 1994

south. The tube-web spider, *Atypus affinis*, was believed extinct for over a century, after its sandy grassland environment changed to woodland and scrub —but it survived where it did probably because the terrain was too steep to mow and rabbits kept it as grassland by eating tree seedlings.

Commented Edward Milner, Spider Recorder for the London Natural History Society: "As I was walking about I was thinking, There's something different around here. Then I started scrabbling around in the grass and saw these webs. On a wet, miserable autumn day I was exhilarated."

The one-inch-long spider gets its name from the tube-shaped web it

WHERE DID I PUT THOSE PENGUINS?

❣ Five penguins were spotted 100 yards off Genoa. Authorities in the Italian port are trying to establish how the birds got there.

❣ Thai customs officials seized a drifting trawler last December. There was no one aboard, apart from "100 young kangaroos and various birds."

❣ A dead bat was found in a pan of frozen broccoli due to be served at a vegetarian lunch at a social services center in Alfreston, England.

❣ Swedish customs in Malmo thought a woman arriving by hovercraft from Copenhagen was too well-endowed. A body search revealed 65 baby grass snakes in her bra and six lizards under her blouse. One lizard, a basilisk, had died in the crush. The 42-year-old said she wanted to start a reptile farm.

❣ A white mongrel dog called John returned bedraggled to his fishing village on Okushiri Island, off Hokkaido, a year after being washed away by a 16-meter tidal wave on July 12, 1993. The wave killed 200 people. John's owner, Naoyuki Iida, said that the dog doesn't like water now but loves eating fish.

❣ Dick Troy awoke on April 20 to find a two-pound Japanese Exotic Carp, with a gash on its back, lying in his garden in Hospital Bridge Road, Twickenham, England. It died in the evening. In June, Mike McCullough was gardening in Woodlake Avenue, Chorlton, near Manchester, when a goldfish landed next to him. He said that no one could have thrown it at him.

❣ Ten policemen and three park rangers, armed with tins of dog food and a soccer goal net, hunted and captured two young wild boar on Wimbledon Common in London. They were sent to a city farm.

❣ A Dutchman who invested more than $900 in a police-trained guard dog to protect his house in Schalkhaar, England, woke up two days later to discover burglars had stolen it.

❣ Rwanda's luxury Hotel Akagera, on the shores of Lake Iliema, has been taken over by buffalo and baboons. Meanwhile in Biera, Mozambique, 30 people have been living in the derelict Trinidade Zoo since the late 1980s. The animals starved to death years ago.

SCHWASCAR

THE SCHWASCAR AWARDS

ANIMAL SUICIDE

❦ Two swallows, returning from their annual migration last spring, discovered that their nest in the eaves of a house in Mudanjiang City, Heilongjiang province, northeast China, had been destroyed, so they built another. The house owner destroyed this one, so they built another. This happened five times. "In extreme despair," according to the *Tianjin Evening News*, "the swallows killed themselves by knocking against the door." In remorse, the owner buried them behind the house.

RUNNERS-UP

❦ Distraught at its owner's death, a collie committed suicide by leaping from a ninth-floor window in Pushkino, near Moscow, on New Year's Eve 1994. The dog spent the entire day lying near its master's coffin. "Then it went onto the balcony and jumped," according to the newspaper *Moskovsky Komsomolets*. Dog and master had been inseparable for years.

❦ Shiraz, a circus lion, killed its Romanian trainer, Elena Tipa, 52, when it locked its jaws round the woman's neck during a performance in Kuwait City in May last year. The lion then starved itself to death "in remorse for killing its trainer," according to the daily *al-Qabas*.

❦ A 12-year-old girl woke up in a village in Roi-et province, Thailand, to find an albino cobra coiled up next to her. She let it "sleep" beside her, but her parents were less sanguine. They called on neighbors who caged the snake and took it to a temple where a monk advised them to "make merit" and release it in the temple grounds. The poor reptile then "committed suicide," according to the tabloid *Thai Rath*. It was thought that snake and girl had known each other in their past lives.

❦ An octopus weighing 58 pounds and with 12-foot limbs was accidentally caught in a lobster trap and was near death when it was donated to the Cabrillo Marine aquarium in Los Angeles in January 1994. On April 11, Octavia, as the creature has been called, was found dead in her 600-gallon tank, which was about six feet wide and four feet deep. During the night, she had wrenched out of her tank a two-inch-diameter drain pipe glued in place and the water had drained away. Animal rights activists said that her natural orange-red color had given way to white, indicating stress, and that she had committed suicide; but Mike Schaadt, exhibits director of the aquarium, said that color changes were not unusual and that Octavia had been feeding well and moving about her tank.

weaves, which is closed at both ends and lies largely below the soil. When beetles, ants and wood lice crawl across its surface, the spider bites through the web and drags the hapless creatures inside.

❤ Another surprise on Hampstead Heath is a strain of crayfish from America in the men's bathing pool. The 10 Louisiana Reds, the size of small lobsters, are the pit-bull terriers of the crayfish world and can deliver a nasty nip. They also carry a plague which could decimate native crayfish. How they arrived is unknown. Fortunately, no female Louisiana Reds have been found in the pond.

CRAB HITCHES RIDE WITH SEAGULL

A one-inch crab turned up 20 miles from the English coast in a garden in Haywards Heath, West Sussex. Hazel Willard of Haylind Road said: "My Labrador, Robbie, just put it on my lap as a gift. I put it in my rockery, but the next morning it had crawled back to my doorstep."

She contacted Brighton Sea Life Centre where the crab, named Shelley, went on display. "I have never heard of a live crab being found so far from the coast," said Mark Anderson of the Sea Life Centre. "He was probably dropped there by a seagull."

BACHELOR BIRD

An errant specimen of Coleridge's "pious bird of good omen," Britain's loneliest and biggest seabird, continues his forlorn search for love at the wrong end of the world. In early April, Albert, a black-browed albatross with an eight-foot wingspan, was back home at Herma Ness on the north coast of Unst in the Shetland Isles after his annual spring search for a mate. The nearest albatross colony is 8,000 miles away in the Falklands. Albert has been observed regularly at Herma Ness for 23 years, and even earlier on the Bass Rock in the Firth of Forth (1967–69). He regularly offers courtship displays to the gannets of Herma Ness, the birds nearest in size and shape, to be met with avian indifference.

COIN-CARRYING COD

Tony Framingham reeled in a 16-pound cod a mile off Dovercourt in Essex, England, and found in its belly a Roman coin, dating from the reign of Emperor Septimus, around 200 A.D.

ATTACKS BY ANIMALS

KILLER WORMS SLOBBER ON SOUTH

This "Planarian vampire," a six-inch-long serial killer, slobbers toxins on victims.

English farmers face many trials, but one of the weirdest is the threat of a predatory alien worm that devours the common earthworm.

This mucus-covered newcomer is four to six inches long, dark purple flecked with brown spots, and has a pale-edged ribbon-like body. The worm is nocturnal and likes to lurk under flower pots and paving stones. It can live a year without eating, but when it does it slobbers all over its prey, which both paralyzes and dissolves its victim. The worm then sucks up the slimy soup.

In the years since 1965, when the New Zealand flatworm *Artioposthia triangulata* was first spotted in Edinburgh's Royal Botanic Garden, the invader has established itself in gardens throughout Scotland and Ireland. The "Planarian vampire" is now looking toward tasty English real estate.

Investigating biologists believe the vector of this invasion is through botanical gardens to garden centers and nurseries, then to domestic gardens and allotments. Teams from the National Museums of Scotland and the Scottish Crop Research Institute in Dundee conducted a two-year survey of hundreds of locations in Scotland. It revealed the full extent of the infestation, which was lowest in farmland. They theorize that this is because there is little mixing of soil between domestic and agricultural land. However, as Clare Putnam wrote in *New Scientist*: "It is sure to infiltrate farmland eventually."

The invader does not burrow—just one reason why the extinction of the native earthworm could have grave consequences for soil fertility and drainage. The flatworm has no natural predator and there is, as yet, no approved chemical deterrent. There are the makings of another ecological disaster.

DERANGED BY DODGY ANCHOVIES

Did the puffins pecking Hitchcock's heroine in The Birds eat addled anchovies for lunch?

The big question left unanswered at the end of Alfred Hitchcock's film *The Birds* was: why did they go wild? Theories have ranged from rabies to the Last

Judgment. But now it seems that the answer might be algae and anchovies.

The genesis of the film seems to date back to 1961 when the small Californian seaside resort of Rio del Mar, near Santa Cruz, was bombarded by hordes of crazed birds. The sooty shearwaters, or puffins, pecked people, smashed into houses and cars, knocked out car headlights, broke windows, chased people around the streets and staggered around vomiting pieces of anchovy over local lawns. Eight people were nipped. Alfred Hitchcock, who was living in nearby Scotts Valley at the time, called the local newspaper for clippings of the event, saying that he was collecting "research materials." Two years later, he made *The Birds,* partly based on a Daphne du Maurier short story and starring Tippi Hedren and Rod Taylor.

At the time, the bird attack was blamed on the foggy weather, which it was believed had disoriented the birds and sent them flying towards the lights of the town. Now David Garrison, a marine biologist at the University of California at Santa Cruz, has discovered a naturally occurring neurotoxin that accounts for their behavior.

NEW YORK'S WILDLIFE

❤ On February 8 a 30-pound, purebred wild female coyote was found dead on the Major Deegan Expressway in the Bronx, not far from Van Cortlandt Park. Another female, weighing 24 pounds, was found shot on February 16 inside the park. A third specimen, this time alive, turned up in Woodlawn Cemetery, where it had been fed for the previous four months by John and Donna Dudar of Yonkers. They only realized it was a coyote after hearing of the dead animals. The authorities planned to take it to a wildlife refuge. A fourth was spotted in Van Cortlandt on February 19. The coyote (*Canis latrans*) is a small cousin of the wolf, native to the American Southwest, which has spread through much of the country in recent decades. They probably entered the Bronx by way of Westchester, where several have been sighted. Van Cortlandt Park, an old Dutch estate of 1,146 acres, is the only viable coyote habitat in the Bronx.

❤ The mutilated carcass of a black bear, a four-foot-tall, 50-pound female, was found on May 22 wrapped in a white blanket in Forest Park, Queens. The bear had been cut open and several organs were removed, including its gall bladder, which could fetch up to $40,000 as an aphrodisiac in China. A crude crucifix was found inside the body, leading police to suspect devotees of the Santeria religion, a mixture of Afro-Caribbean theology and Catholicism, involving animal sacrifice. But it turned out that the cross was a gesture of sorrow by 12-year-old animal lover Eric Suarez. "I didn't want other animals to eat it, so I put the cross there to protect it," he said.

❤ Pigs and wild boar were roaming New York City on June 14. Two white pigs were caught on wasteland in Queens in the morning and two wild boars on Staten Island in the afternoon, with a third one dead, run over by a car. A fourth boar was lassoed on June 16.

LOVE HURTS

❤ Returning home from working the night shift in January 1995, an unnamed police officer at Stone, Staffordshire, England, couldn't resist making passionate advances toward his wife as she was making breakfast. He proceeded to wrap a slice of bread around his penis, at which point his hungry pet Labrador took one look at the hot dog on display and took a swift bite. The man, in his twenties, was left rolling on the floor. He was off sick for several days and needed cosmetic surgery. A fellow officer stated that his doctor banned him from sex for a few weeks, and that everyone was waiting to see how he filled out his sick form.

❤ Spurned lover Marco Zagni of Milan tried to win back his former girlfriend Louisa Pietra in 1987 by swinging Tarzan-style into her bedroom on a rope attached to a pylon. He smashed through the window and knocked himself unconscious. Louisa was unsympathetic. "How could I marry someone so stupid?" she said.

❤ Army officer Major Donald Schneider romantically swept his wife Deborah off her feet to carry her into their hotel room in Fort Leavenworth, Kansas, in November 1989. Unfortunately she was wearing a fur coat, which made her hard to grip, and when she started to fidget he tripped and dropped her over a three-foot-high wooden railing. On the other side was an eight-floor drop into the hotel lobby. Deborah landed on a restaurant table, breaking both legs and her pelvis in the 75-foot fall.

In 1991 he noticed that groups of pelicans and cormorants gathering on the coast near the campus seemed "intoxicated, swimming in circles and squawking pitifully." Hundreds of corpses were collected over the next few weeks. Dr. Garrison isolated domoic acid from the corpses and found that it had accumulated in the bodies of the birds after they had gorged on shoals of anchovies which had in turn fed on the algae that had "bloomed" in Monterey Bay.

Domoic acid is produced by a phytoplankton called *Pseudo-nitzschia australis* when it runs low on vital nutrients. It accumulates in shrimp, fish, crabs and the seabirds that feed on them. In high concentrations it causes vomiting, severe dementia, extreme aggressiveness and ultimately death. In 1987, for instance, more than 100 people living on Prince Edward Island in Canada fell ill after eating mussels contaminated with domoic acid. Four died. Although such outbreaks are rare, Garrison discovered that there are twice-yearly blooms of the algae in Monterey Bay, each lasting several weeks. The Rio del Mar outbreak in 1961 was at the right time of year for such a bloom, although the case will probably never be proved conclusively. It is not known why so few of these blooms lead to domoic acid poisoning.

REST IN BEAST

Kenyan Member of Parliament Chris Kamuyu proposed that hyenas be used to clean up hospitals with no mortuaries by eating the bodies of the unclaimed dead. A fellow MP had complained his district hospital had no public cemetery.

MIDNIGHT CREEPERS

Ugly but harmless marine wood lice swarmed south London in February.

Thousands of unfamiliar cockroach-like insects swarmed over the Globe Industrial Estate in Woolwich, south London, on February 15. Almost two inches long and waving grotesque antenna, they were identified as harmless *Ligia oceanica* (marine wood lice), carried beyond their usual haunts by a freak flood tide. "They really do look like something out of a horror movie," said entomologist Jim Brock, "but they are common enough around coastal areas and will not stray from salt water, although they can't actually swim. They generally live in crevices and are nocturnal. They eat fungi or decaying wood."

EXPENSIVE TASTES

An ostrich called Clyde was found with a $1,600 diamond in his throat after a postmortem examination in Nebraska. The seven-foot bird had choked to death trying to eat the contents of a jewelry box.

DELINQUENT DOLPHINS

Despite their friendly reputation, bottle-nosed dolphins have been savaging their porpoise cousins in the Moray Firth off northeast Scotland. Vets' suspicions were raised when they found that 42 out of 105 porpoise carcasses from around Scotland between 1991 and 1993 had suffered severe internal in-

BEWARE OF BEASTS

❧ Crows have been tormenting Moscow, sliding down the shining gold cupolas of the Kremlin and destroying the ancient gilt with their claws. Reproductions of crows' warning cries have failed so far to frighten them away.

❧ A hungry hippo wreaked havoc along the Niger River in West Africa, attacking canoes and destroying rice fields. Villagers in Mali hunted the animal in vain. Many believed that the hippo had magical powers of flight and invisibility.

❧ A crocodile attacked Robert Minihan in the Baramundi Gorge, northern Australia, in July, but he survived. Mr. Minihan is a chef who specializes in crocodile dishes.

❧ A rare griffon vulture with a six-foot wingspan attacked the referee and players at a soccer match on Tenerife in the Canaries. Injuries were not serious and the game resumed after the bird's departure. The report in *Ivoir'Soir* blamed sorcery by the opposing team.

ANIMAL SABOTEURS

❣ The launch of the space shuttle *Discovery* was delayed from June 8 to July 13 when NASA discovered that two woodpeckers had made 135 holes, up to four inches in diameter, in the fuel tank's insulating foam. Technicians had to move the shuttle from the launch pad so that they could patch up all the holes, at a cost of nearly $100,000. The Kennedy Space Center is in a wildlife refuge. When the delayed countdown commenced, ground controllers serenaded the astronauts with Woody Woodpecker's trademark snicker.

❣ The Daya Bay nuclear power plant in Shenzhen, China, was opened in February 1994 and supplies much of Hong Kong's electricity. By November, however, it was faced with a major threat to safety as white ants went on a rampage, chewing through everything in sight. The ants had been busy in Shenzhen, eating banknotes, invading a reservoir, closing an electronics factory and blacking out a hotel.

❣ A porcupine in South Africa chomped through a bunch of buried fiber optic cables, cutting off a large number of telephones in the Vereeninging area south of Johannesburg. A trail of fragments led engineers to the porcupine's lair.

❣ A squirrel wiped out power to Derby City Hospital in England and more than 1,100 houses when it climbed a power line and touched an 11,000-volt cable in October 1994. Two months later, a possum caused a huge blackout for an hour on the north side of Brisbane, Australia, by crawling into a substation and shorting a 110-kilovolt line.

juries. Some also had knife-like marks on their skin which exactly matched the spacing of dolphin teeth. While dolphins fight each other to establish a social hierarchy, this run of attacks on porpoises has allegedly never before been recorded.

Another case of dolphin aggression occurred on December 8, 1994, when Joao Paulo Moreira and Wilson Reis Pedroso tried to ride a dolphin and tie objects to its tail. The dolphin, a tourist attraction at a beach in Caraguatatuba, 200 miles southwest of Rio de Janeiro, nicknamed Tiao (short for Sebastiao), responded to this presumption with some repeated head-butting. Moreira died of massive internal bleeding and Pedroso was treated for a broken rib. Three days later, at the weekend, Tiao

turned on seven other swimmers. One 37-year-old man suffered internal injuries and was in critical condition. One can sympathize with the normally gentle dolphin: it is constantly approached by swimmers, some of whom attempt to feed it beer or put ice cream down its breathing hole. The local mayor resisted calls for Tiao's capture.

....

DEATH ON THE HOOF

....

Josef Meschede, a farmer from Augsburg, Germany, was charged with murdering his wife by training his bull to attack on command. He lured Karolina, 40, to the concrete paddock where Maxi was kept, hit her on the head with a pitchfork and gave the command to kill.

Police became suspicious when Josef, 44, tried to cash in $750,000 worth of life insurance policies. They also discovered that he had contacted dating agencies before his wife died.

BOVINE BETROTHAL?

Israel Zinhanga, 28, had sex with a cow because he was afraid of contracting AIDS from a human partner. A Zimbabwe court sentenced him to nine months. He said he was in love with the cow and pledged to be faithful to her during his imprisonment.

FOXY HOUNDS HOUNDED

The fox was soon forgotten when an all-male East Dulverston pack of hounds picked up the scent of 30 broody bitches from the Exmoor hunt in Somerset, England. It took huntsmen over an hour to break up the orgy.

POOPER SCOOPED

Margaret Roythorne looked on in horror as her tiny Cairn terrier Fynn was sucked up and killed by a mobile "pooper-scooper" in her local park in Hastings, England. The seven-year-old dog was run over by the vacuum muck-collector after dashing out from some bushes.

PECULIAR PRESS

GIANT MOUSTACHE HOVERS OVER CITY
Independent (London), June 21, 1994

MAD DUCK STOLE MY TROUSERS SAYS OAP
Bedfordshire Times, June 24, 1994

LABRADOR PUPS ON WAY TO COMBAT CRIME IN RUSSIA
Western Mail, June 17, 1994

ATTACKS ON ANIMALS

BIRDS DINE ON BIRDS

A Mauritius kestrel, one of the world's rarest falcons, has eaten one of the world's rarest pigeons. The kestrel pounced on the Mauritius pink pigeon on the Ile aux Aigrettes, off the coast of Mauritius. The breeding program of the Jersey Wildlife Preservation Trust managed to bring back the falcon population from four birds 18 years ago to its present 250. The trust had a similar success with the pigeons, which were dying out through deforestation and the introduction of predators such as monkeys.

A month later, thousands of bird-watchers raced to Languard in Suffolk to catch a glimpse of the beautiful Blyth's Pipit, blown off course from Siberia and only the third reported sighting in Britain this century. As they

STRANGE DEATHS

❦ In the Ukraine, three 18-year-olds doing national service were sent to clean a 12-foot-deep underground food container in Charkov. They were fatally overcome by pickled-cabbage fumes, as was a 48-year-old worker who went to their rescue.

❦ Welfare clerk James Chenault, 54, boarded a lift in the Kingsbridge Welfare Center in the Bronx, New York, with four others on January 6, 1995. The lift raced up to the second floor, apparently out of control. When the doors opened, Chenault straddled the doorway to allow the others off. One made it out, but with the doors still open, the lift resumed its climb, decapitating Chenault. His head, wearing stereo headphones, fell into the lift with the three remaining passengers while his body fell down the shaft.

❦ Jilted lover Edward Hand, trying to commit suicide, fired a bullet into his chin. The slug ricocheted off his teeth, out of his right cheek and into the head of his rival Ronald Gauley, 34, killing him. It took investigators almost four months to figure out what had happened, but they finally arrested Hand, 33, and charged him with third-degree murder. The shooting was the result of a triangle involving Hand, Gauley and Gauley's wife, Kathy. Gauley and his wife separated in 1993 and Kathy Gauley moved in with Hand. In June 1994, she moved out and talked about reuniting with her husband. At a tavern called The Twilight Zone, the three met to talk things over on September 23. They all wound up at Hand's trailer in Bartow, 30 miles east of Tampa, Florida, where the incident happened.

❦ A police officer at Cairo's main station noticed blood running down the side of a train on February 22 and discovered a human head on the roof. The rest of the body was found 60 miles away, on the ground near the bridge which had decapitated Mohamed Zaher Abderrahman, 22, in the Nile delta town of Kafr al-Zayyat.

took photographs, a kestrel snatched the pipit in its claws and flew off.

PULSELESS PET

Notice seen in New Zealand's *Ashburton Guardian:* "Wanted—Child's first pony. Must be very quiet, faultless and nearly dead."

HOLE IN ONE

Peter Croke whacked his golf ball down the fairway and saw it shoot straight up the rear end of a grazing sheep.

The startled ewe bolted off towards the 17th green as Peter and his partner John Maher collapsed laughing. To their astonishment, the ball dropped out on the footpath 30 yards closer to the green, helping Peter to win the match.

Peter, a deputy headmaster from Crowbridge in South Glamorgan, had fluffed his drive on the 17th at Southerndown golf club near Porthcawl, Mid Glamorgan, and his shot scored a bull's-eye in the sheep 40 yards away. As the beast sauntered off unharmed, Peter played the ball from where it dropped and won by a stroke.

Peter didn't know the rules covering sheep's rear-ends, so he checked back at the clubhouse. Officials ruled he had been right to hit the ball where it landed because the animal had been in bounds.

RABID RUSSIAN

A drunk man of 37 seized hold of Elsa, an Alsatian dog that jumped at him in a park in the Ukrainian city of Denpropetrovsk. He then sank his teeth into its throat and bit it to death in front of its owner.

IT'S RAINING WHALE BLUBBER

The Great Exploding Whale of Oregon story has already gained legendary status on the Internet. Regularly queried, it is now enshrined in the Frequently Asked Questions (FAQ) of the alt.folklore.urban newsgroup—and as several *FT* readers have asked about it, it is time to record it in these pages.

The story concerns an attempt by engineers from the Oregon State Highway Division to remove a 45-foot, eight-ton dead whale from an Oregon beach by blowing it up, hoping that seagulls would feast on the pieces. The event was filmed for a local TV news show, but no one is quite sure who digitized the footage and made it available.

One netter, Tom Mahoney, posted this summary of the climax: "So they moved the spectators back up the beach, put a half-ton of dynamite next to the whale and set it off.... First you see the whale carcass disappear in a huge blast of smoke and flame. Then you hear the happy spectators shouting 'Yayyy!' and 'Wheee!' Then, suddenly, the crowd's tone changes. You hear a new sound—like 'splud.' You hear a woman's voice shouting 'Here come pieces of... my God!' Something smears the camera lens."

The humor of the situation—such as it was—suddenly gave way to a run for cover as huge chunks of whale blubber spludded. One piece was said to have caved in the roof of a car parked more than a quarter of a mile away. The bulk of the whale made a sagging bridge across a huge crater and there was not a seagull in sight.

It was hailed as "the most wonderful event in the history of the universe," and news that it could be downloaded from a site on the Net spread quickly. Somehow the story spread faster than the site address and before long, this "wonderful event" was regarded—even beyond the pale of the Net—as just another folktale.

In many ways the oddest aspect of the Exploding Whale saga is the impression that dynamiting dead whales is rare or bizarre—indeed it is often the most practical way of quickly removing what is a galloping health hazard. One netter, Martin Adamson, recently explained that "Here in Scotland, it is standard practice for the Coast Guard to blow up beached dead whales. This happens three to four times a year. They are too big to dispose of otherwise. The fragments are then bulldozed and buried."

The story, as told, certainly had the hallmarks of an urban legend: no names, no date, and human stupidity backfiring semi-humorously with grim results. Following several years' relegation by net.lorists to the "false" category, it was pointed out that the story could have been derived from a humorous column by American journalist Dave Barry. Then it became clear that Barry was describing the same event that was filmed and the long-awaited archive locations were posted.

If you have a modem, an Internet connection and the know-how, you can download the 11.7 megabyte film file by anonymous FTP from the following sites: stirling.dorm.umd.edu directory /pub/whale.avi, and dixie.aiss.uiuc.edu directory pub/cathouse/urban.legend/gif/ul/whale.avi.

The video clip lasts nearly three minutes. It is a bit jerky and pixelated but, as another netter commented: "It's worth it.... Once you've watched it, you can take an authoritative standpoint on whale detonation....The shot of the actual explosion is cool, and yes, you do actually hear the 'spluds' of blubber landing around the camera crew." *FT* was disappointed, though, that nothing 'spluds' across the camera lens.

Captions in the clip reveal that it was filmed by a Doug Brazil at Florence in Oregon. We have no further details on file about it, but there is no doubting the authenticity of the film.

SWARMINGS

BEES PAY LAST RESPECTS

Human and insect friends of late beekeeper Margaret Bell assembled after her funeral.

Mrs. Margaret Bell, who kept bees in Leintwardine about seven miles from her home in Ludlow, England, died in June this year. Her funeral service in Ludlow was rounded off with one of her favorite hymns, "All Things Bright and Beautiful." Soon afterwards, mourners were astonished to see a swarm of hundreds of bees settle on the corner of Bell Lane, directly opposite 42 Mill Street where Mrs. Bell had lived for the last 26 years. The bees stayed for about an hour before buzzing off over the rooftops. "I think it is absolutely wonderful that they should stop opposite her house," said Mrs. Bell's friend, Sue Walsh. According to country lore, you should always tell the bees when someone has died so they can come and say goodbye.

NOT ALL FUNERAL–GOING
BEES ARE SO KIND:

A swarm of killer bees that attended a funeral on September 7, 1994, in Concepcion del Oro, Mexico, stung 140 mourners.

SICKLY CRITTERS

❧ Katanda, a six-year-old okapi, a member of the giraffe family, started hyperventilating, collapsed and died in Copenhagen Zoo on August 5 when performers at the Royal Theatre began rehearsing selections from Wagner's *Tannhauser* in a park 300 yards away. The corpse was sent to Copenhagen University for stuffing, but was stolen and barbecued by students.

❧ Farmhand Paulo Golart found bricks of plastic-wrapped marijuana hidden in a farm pen near Poto Alegre, Brazil. Thinking it was strong-smelling alfalfa, he fed it to a cow and three heifers, who died of overdoses.

❧ A mystifying outbreak of blindness among kangaroos in New South Wales in June 1994 led to the bounders blundering into trees.

❧ In a report in *Audubon* magazine, Ursula de Garza of the border town of Matamoros, Mexico, said her dogs no longer have a flea problem. "We grab the dogs and stick them in the canal [that connects several chemical companies] and the fleas are gone. All the hair falls off too, but gradually it comes back."

THE SCHWASCAR AWARDS

SCHWASCAR

ANIMAL SABOTAGE

❧ On April 4, 1993, a crow caused the total stoppage of a turbine at the Ignalima power station in Lithuania by landing on a 330-kilowatt pylon with a piece of electric cable in its beak, short-circuiting the power. The turbine was only stopped for a short period, but the crow was fried to a crisp.

RUNNERS-UP:

❧ Nobody saw the bird that blacked out more than 9,000 homes in Newbridge, England at 8 P.M. one evening in mid-April 1994. The only evidence was a five-day-old lamb, found fried in a field beneath 11,000-volt cables. Ornithologists suggested that an escaped eagle swooped on the lamb at dusk, but dropped its supper over the power lines.

❧ In August 1993, a 12-foot, 44-pound python slithered through three security grilles at a Vietnamese hydroelectric plant and blocked a pressure pipeline, causing a turbine to explode. Another turbine at the plant was damaged by flooding and power supplies to the city of Pleiku were disrupted.

❧ Rats are bringing chaos to Moscow by gnawing through traffic light cables faster than they can be repaired, the *Rossyiskaya Gazette* reported.

❧ The second largest stock market in the United States was halted for 34 minutes on August 1, 1994, when a squirrel chewed into power lines near the Nasdaq computer center at Trumbull, Connecticut. Though Nasdaq never lost power completely, automatic systems tried in vain to switch over to a standby generator.

❧ An army of cockroaches was found sabotaging telephones in the local government ministry headquarters in Harare, Zimbabwe, in February 1993. Technicians, called in after scores of complaints about unanswered calls, discovered thousands of cockroaches "milling about inside the switchboard."

❧ A bird dropped a rosy boa snake over an electricity substation west of Twentynine Palms, California, blacking out more than 4,000 homes in the high desert Morongo Basin for two hours on May 11, 1994.

❧ Repeated blackouts in 40 houses in Lepton, England, were traced to a Shire horse, Dolly Blue, and her thoroughbred friends, JR, Billy Whiz and Tommy Sausage, who were scratching themselves on cables supporting an electric pole in their field. The vibrations caused overhead wires to touch each other.

NEW SPECIES FOUND

KILLER SPONGE

The first flesh-eating sponges have been found in a Mediterranean sea cave, 60 feet below the surface, some 18 miles from Marseilles. The sponge, belonging to the genus *Asbestopluma,* grows to an inch or so in length and uses tendrils covered with hook-like spicules, the equivalent of Velcro, to trap crustaceans and drag them down. Fresh filaments grow over the prey and digestion takes several days.

Dr. Jean Vacelet, who made the discovery and wrote it up with Dr. Nicole Boury-Estnault in *Nature* (January 1995), said that *Asbestopluma* held the depth record for sponges and had been found 29,000 feet down in the Pacific. The cave was home to several deep sea animals because it trapped colder waters typical of great depths. Many such animals were carnivores because of the poverty of their habitat.

TWO LUVARS CAUGHT

The first ever live specimen of the Luvar fish, *Luvarus Imperialis,* was netted off the Azores in late June 1994 by the Cornish trawler *Britannia Four.* The 42-pound healthy specimen was bought by a Swansea fishmonger who decided to donate it to science when he realized how rare it was. Looking like a cross between a dolphin and a tuna, its dark blue back is dotted with pink spots, tapering to a shiny silver underneath, while the tail and fins are a vivid crimson. It was due to be sent to the Marine Biological Association in Plymouth for study.

The Luvar fish is normally found in waters between 200 and 1,000 feet deep and was first identified in 1866. The Natural History Museum had only seen five specimens this century. Until last summer, the fullest account of its bone structure, published in America in 1943, was based on a single dried skeleton so shrunk that its length could not be estimated. It eats jellyfish, but it is not known how it breeds or whether it migrates.

Less than a month later, a second specimen was brought into Newlyn harbor. It had been caught by Chris Hill, skipper of *Ar Bageergan,* and was passed to the Natural History Museum.

HERMAPHROGOAT

Mufeed Scheikh holds up a $50 glass of his mutant goat's magic milk.

Palestinian farmer Mufeed Scheikh from Siniria, near Tulkarem on the West Bank, had a "golden billy goat" that developed a milk-bearing udder.

ANIMAL AFFECTIONS

IN A SNAILSPIN

💀 This curious photograph by Bob Barrs appeared in the Harborne Gazette, a free paper from the Birmingham area, in August 1994. A snail had been squashed in a local garden and around its remains another snail had made an unbroken circle of slime and continued to follow the same circular path. Three hours later, it was still going round and round and the slime was so thick it formed a "platform."

A naturalist speculated that the crushed snail was emitting pheromones which attracted the second snail. The first part of the snail's courtship ritual consists of going round in circles, followed by an exchange of "love darts." In this case, the darts never came. Happily, it began to rain and presumably the pheromones were washed away. The snail stopped circling and slithered off into the undergrowth.

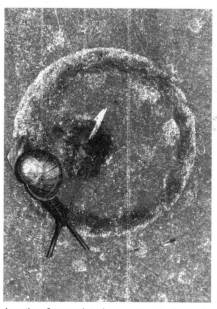

A snail performs a three-hour mating ritual around its squashed friend.

THE RAT SAT ON THE CAT

This curious cat defends his mouse friend.

💀 A pet white rat and Oscar, a feral cat, both inmates of an animal welfare center at Mellerstain in the Scottish borders, became the best of friends. The rat was missing from its cage one day and was found cuddled up to Oscar. "We thought the cat must have killed him," said the assistant manager. "But when we gave him a poke he just looked at us, blinked a couple of times, pulled the cat's tail around him and went back to sleep. It is a very strange thing because the cat spits and scratches at us and feral cats live on mice and rats and other things they can kill and eat."

He sold the milk for $50 a glass as tales spread that the freak of nature, named Abu Mosa'id ("The Father of Hope"), had magical powers and could cure impotence and sterility. It certainly solved the financial problems of its owner, who was cut off from his construction job in Israel when the government sealed off the West Bank and Gaza Strip after a terrorist attack in January.

The goat was a male in every respect—the animal had sired 50 kids—except for one teat, which gave just two glasses of milk a day. Mufeed fed the goat on a special diet of fruit and vegetables, but slaughtered it when he could no longer stand the pressure of masses of people descending on his sleepy village. He denied rumors that the Islamic Resistance Movement (Hamas) had forced him to kill the animal to maintain public order.

TASMANIAN TIGER SIGHTING

Charlie Beasley, a part-time ranger with the Tasmanian Parks and Wildlife Service, is quite certain that the animal he saw through binoculars at dusk on January 25, inland from St. Helen's in northeastern Tasmania, was a Thylacine, or Tasmanian tiger. "What I viewed for two minutes was about half the size of a fully-matured German shepherd dog, with stripes over his body from about halfway down, and a tail curved like a kangaroo's," he said. "He sniffed the ground, lifted his head and ran into the bush. He was a scrappy color like a dingo—that horrible sandy color that looks like he needed a bath."

No tracks were found, as the ground was too hard. The sighting came just in time; the Tasmanian government had decided to end all funding for Thylacine research, which had been about

MASS DEATHS

PORPOISE PILE-UP

❦ Nineteen fit and healthy dolphins beached themselves and died near Ross Point in County Mayo, western Ireland, on September 19, 1994, possibly because they followed a dominant male that appeared to have suffered heart failure. Sick cetaceans often beach themselves. This was the largest recorded stranding of Atlantic white-sided dolphins, which live in open water and rarely venture inshore. Reports of stranded cetaceans have increased in recent years, possibly caused by growing marine pollution or novel diseases such as the distemper that killed thousands of seals in 1988.

LAMBS TO THE SLAUGHTER

❦ A herd of sheep committed mass suicide in a lake in Inner Mongolia on July 17, refusing to return to shore despite frantic efforts by their Chinese shepherd to save them. Two goats with an apparent death wish jumped into the five-foot-deep water, prompting the rest to follow. After a three-hour rescue aided by 20 herdsmen, the shepherd succeeded in saving 281 sheep while the other 249 animals, including 206 goats, drowned. Some of the rescued animals tried to jump back in. Veterinary experts had no explanation for this unusual behavior and an inquiry was planned.

$1,000 a year for the last decade. Now a few more hundred dollars will probably be allocated for wildlife officer Nick Mooney to follow up the sighting. The last undoubted Thylacine died in Hobart Zoo in 1934.

....

RETURN OF THE WOOLLY JUMPER

....

The woolly flying squirrel, *Eupetaurus cinereus,* was discovered in the Himalayas in 1888. After a few technical papers and a single anecdotal account of a live, captive animal, the last known sighting was in 1924 and the species was believed extinct. Some zoologists suspected otherwise, however. Peter Zahler and Chantal Dietemann from Watertown, New York, have spent many months in the valleys of Kashmir since 1992 looking for the animal. Their perseverance paid off last summer in the Sai Valley near Gilgit in Pakistan when Ms. Dietemann found a front paw, apparently torn from the leg of a woolly flying squirrel by a predator.

A few days later, two local men appeared and claimed to be collectors of salagit, an allegedly aphrodisiac and medicinal substance sold in Gilgit—and which was said to be the crystallized urine of the woolly flying squirrel. Six hours later, they returned to collect their $150 finder's fee, with a female specimen in a sack. The collection site,

NUKING THE POODLE

❂ John Celinski, 33, a NASA subcontractor from Texas, dosed two cats with the pain reliever acetaminophen and microwaved them, after which they died. He was jealous of the cats, Sugar Ray and Bonnie, which belonged to his girlfriend Sheryl Jones. On September 8, 1994, the Harris County District Court fined him $1,800 with two years' probation.

❂ In 1985 in Bournemouth, England, a Lebanese student was cleared of cruelly ill-treating Boo-Boo, his landlady's budgie, which died after being put in a microwave oven. Magistrates heard a tape recording made at the time in which Yehia el-Zahran, 23, could be heard laughing hysterically as the bird chirped its last. Of course, one might ask why a recording had been made and why the cackling el-Zahran was acquitted (self-defense? justifiable avicide?) but Fortean researchers learn to live with puzzles such as these.

❂ In 1990, an Ontario court sentenced Melissa Weiler, 20, to three years' probation for killing her roommate's cat by cooking it in a microwave oven. In 1992, lawyer Stanley Protowicz helped a client break into his wife's home. He then guzzled champagne and stuffed the cat in the microwave. He told a court in Maryland that the oven was turned on "by mistake"—but he was fined $1,000.

❂ A Californian girl, aged 13, was arrested in 1991, accused of housebreaking and torturing pets, often to death, including baking a cat in a microwave. The unnamed cutie had ripped birds apart, smearing their blood on walls. She had also shaved dogs and saturated them with household chemicals. Another trick was taking dogs from one house and switching them with dogs from another. Obscenities and gang-related messages were spray-painted on walls.

where the animal was later released, was a cave high up on an extremely steep and rocky slope. The creature is two feet tall, sports a two-foot-long tail and is the largest living member of the squirrel family. Its cry is said to herald the death of a loved one.

NEW MAMMAL IN 'NAM

An unknown large mammal, the "forest goat," *Vu Quang Ox*, or *sao la* ("weaving spindle," so named because of its horns) was identified from skulls and antlers in 1992 found in the Vu Quang Nature Reserve, a mountainous rainforest on the border of Vietnam and Laos. The animal has similarities to the African and Arabian oryx—but has its own genus, *Pseudoryx nghentinhensis*, the second part after the province's former name.

The first Pseudoryx calf is snapped eating leaves in its cage near Hanoi, Vietnam.

In June 1994, in the Khe Tre Watershed Forest just outside Vu Quang, a local tortoise hunter stumbled upon a live *sao la* which was caught by his dogs. It was a female calf about five months old, weighing just over 40 pounds and standing two feet tall at the shoulder. It hadn't developed the straight 18-inch horns, which were under two inches long. (Adults weigh up to 225 pounds and stand about three feet tall.) Kept in a botanic garden outside Hanoi, it

ANIMAL ANOMALIES

❦ Kolya the crocodile has died in the Urals city of Ekaterinburg. He arrived in the town between 1913 and 1915 as part of a touring animal show. He was already full-grown then, suggesting he was between 110 and 115 when he died.

❦ A chicken in western Iran has set a record for laying an egg on average nearly every hour. Jalil Khorshidi of Kermnshah told the IRNA news agency that the chicken had laid 42 eggs in a 52-hour period.

❦ A foot-long marsupial called Gilbert's potoroo, last sighted in 1869, has been discovered in a nature reserve near Albany on the southern coast of Western Australia—five adults including two females with tiny young in their pouches. Genetic study will ascertain if the animal is a sub-species of the long-nosed potoroo—or a distinct species.

❦ Two male storks built a nest together in a zoo in Osnabrück, Germany, and hatched a discarded penguin's egg.

gained weight on a diet of milk, bananas and corn. It had distinctive white markings on its face and hooves, large eyes, a short fluffy tail and a thin blackish-brown stripe down the middle of its back. A second specimen, about six months old, 32 inches tall and three feet long, was captured in July, but by October one had died from diarrhea, the other from liver and bladder problems. There may be only a few hundred left and scientists fear that the *sao la* may be hunted to extinction before it has been properly studied.

TERRIBLE TERMITES

The termite *Reticulitermes lucifugus,* normally found in southern Europe and North Africa, has arrived in England. A colony was discovered in two timber-frame walls, heated by pipes, in a bungalow in Saunton, near Barnstaple in Devon.

"The timber was damp and the combination of heat and moisture has produced the perfect microclimate," said Roger Berry of the Building Research Establishment. "It would seem they have been there for several years." He believes they were probably imported in a plant or in packaging. Investigators counted at least 500 insects in "just one foot of skirting board."

Meanwhile, concrete-crunching termites are causing more than $4.5 million in damage every year to modern buildings in Chengdu, capital of China's western Sichuan province. Tiny white insects, previously thought to be a threat only to wooden buildings, adapted to urban life and can bore through reinforced concrete and damage objects made of copper, iron and aluminum.

SHRIMPLY UNBELIEVABLE

THE WORLD'S FAVORITE CRUSTACEAN HAS BEEN GIVING THE ZOOLOGISTS A FEW SURPRISES LATELY:

The mulching mouth of this prehistoric seven-foot shrimp struck fear in smaller sea life.

❧ New evidence suggests that *Anomalocaris* ("Odd Shrimp"), which thrived 525 million years ago, long before any life on land, was a fearsome marine monster that grew up to seven feet long and had a mouth like a mulching machine for consuming trilobites and other trifles. Fish, as we know them, were not around. This king prawn ruled the world.

❧ A colony of translucent shrimps has survived in total darkness 1,080 feet below ground in a sulfurous puddle at Tyneside's Wearmouth colliery in England since 1826, eating only coal dust, sulphur-eating bacteria and crumbs of bread thrown to them by miners.

Fifty of the half-inch, blind shellfish, along with bottles of "coal dust soup," have been rescued by Dr. Phil Gates of Durham University, who hopes to maintain a breeding colony in the university labs. "You can see the black gut which is the coal passing through their digestive system," he said. "It's possible that they are a new species, but more likely that they have adapted independently into a subspecies." Dietary advice was available from Wearmouth shaftman Ken Drysdale, who has fed the colony four times a week since 1979. The colliery was due to be filled in this summer.

❧ A "living fossil" was discovered in June 1993 living deep in caves at Wee Jasper, 44 miles west of Canberra, Australia. It is an invertebrate syncarid much like a shrimp and dates back to the supercontinent of Gondwanaland when Africa, South America and Australia were one landmass.

❧ A shrimp-like creature, found only on the Pacific beaches of Panama and seen by only a handful of people, invented wheeled transport millions of years before the Sumerians did in about 3,000 B.C. The one-inch-long creature "forms its body into a wheel and then rolls along as if it were a hoop," said Professor Roy Caldwell of the University of California at Berkeley.

MISPLACED ANIMAL PARTS

❧ In early December 1994, a Boeing 737-400 returned to its Istanbul base from Stockholm after an uneventful charter flight. The maintenance crew were puzzled to find that the aircraft's leading edge, at a point just outboard of the engine, was contaminated by crabs' legs.

❧ Ken Chenoweth from Bristol, England, who has a snake phobia, found rattlesnake bones in a packet of peanuts; and Ken Cope from Witney, Oxfordshire, found a bone from a child's hand in a packet of pistachio nuts.

❧ Firemen were called to a gas leak in Mile End, east London, caused by a split barrel of bull's semen. The semen was preserved in nitrogen and it exploded when the barrel fell off a truck.

❧ Hundreds of headless seagulls were washed up on a beach in Poole, England, in July. A spokesman for Dorset Wildlife Trust commented: "I find it difficult to imagine natural circumstances decapitating birds. It could be mink, but sadly it is always possible that it was done by human beings."

❧ About 100 crocodile skulls were dug up last summer in Western Australia about 60 miles east of Narrogin. Some of the snouts were tagged, indicating that they were from a crocodile park; but the nearest such park was in Freemantle, over 120 miles away.

❧ One hundred and fifty pigs' heads have been found by residents in the Tokyo suburb of Omiya in 16 separate incidents. Police are baffled as the meat from such heads is considered a delicacy. The finds have grown exponentially since 1992, when five cases were reported.

DEMENTED ANIMAL ATTACK

❦ A herd of wild elephants, intoxicated by the smell of liquor, smashed through a house in Midnapore district, West Bengal, India, and trampled to death a man brewing moonshine. Elephants frequently get blotto on rum or fermented fruit, but death is seldom the outcome.

RUNNERS-UP

❦ A Holstein cow stepped on the trigger of a loaded rifle left in a field by a farm worker near the town of Velez, about 150 miles north of Bogota, Colombia. The rifle went off, sending a bullet straight into the head of another cow grazing nearby. The victim's condition was critical. We haven't heard if she pulled through.

❦ A cow crashed through the roof of a house cut into a hill in Yaounde, Cameroon, and landed on the dinner table at midnight as Marguerite Nomo, 23, was watching *Dances with Wolves* on TV. She fled, believing that the cow was a black magic "warning."

❦ Doctors in a Mexican hospital were in the midst of open-heart surgery when a frog fell out of an overhead lamp and landed on the patient, according to the *Daily Star*.

❦ Twelve cats on a farm in Floresville, Texas, were stung to death on November 3, 1994, by African "killer" bees. "They covered the cats' faces and bodies," said Tillie Dziuk, 63. "The bees ate out the eyes and got in the nostrils, so the cats couldn't breathe. I've never seen anything like it in my life."

❦ Great horned owls get hungry when snow covers their normal prey, and one terrorized a pensioners' housing development in Greenville, Maine, in January 1994. "When people tried to get out of their houses it would swoop down on them," said Paul Fournier of the Department of Inland Fisheries and Wildlife. "People were afraid to go out." The owl was the prime suspect in the disappearance of cats and had stripped the neighborhood of squirrels and birds. Robert Shufelt said the owl attacked his dog, Bandit, when he took it outside on January 4, 1995. It lifted the 20-pound poodle-Pekinese crossbreed into the air and out of sight. Moments later, the dog dropped dead from the sky. A game warden shot the pesky bird the next day.

❦ Swarms of crows have been attacking farm animals near Potsdam, Germany. "For weeks they live with the herd, then all of a sudden they pounce on the animals," said Norbert Droese, a farmer in Kienberg. "The defenseless beasts don't have a chance—usually calves, or cows that have just given birth." Droese had seen the birds claw out the animals' eyes, then tear them apart, right down to the spinal column. The attacks usually happen on cloudy mornings.

MANIMALS

CHINA'S WILDMAN

The hunt for China's *yeren* or "wildman" has been pursued since 1959, with more than 200 reported sightings. Footprints, samples of hair and feces have been obtained, but no creatures captured or photographed. The latest publicized sighting was in September 1993, when a group of Chinese engineers saw three of them roaming the trails of the Shennongjia National Forest Park in western Hubei province. A local rumor that the son of a wildman and a shy human mother lived in seclusion in the mountains turned out to have been based solely on a videotape of a naked microcephalic man (a "pinhead") eating a banana.

On October 27, 1994, the Chinese government set up a new body, the Committee for the Search of Strange and Rare Creatures, one of whose aims was to investigate wildman reports. Its members included scientists from the Institute of Vertebrate Palæontology and Palæanthropology of the Chinese Academy of Sciences. The wildmen are thought to be unknown primates. The largest cast of a footprint is 16 inches long, leading to the assumption that the creatures could weigh as much as 660 pounds and stand more than 7 feet tall. The committee has studied eight hair specimens, believed to come from animals ranging throughout China and Tibet—none, they say, come from humans or any known animal. The hair varies from black, collected in Yunnan province, to white from Tibet, to the reddish brown of the creatures seen by Hubei villagers.

A 30-strong wildman expedition set out for the mountains of Hubei on April 7, led by Professor Yuan Zhengxin, chairman of the new committee. "I am certain that within three years we will have captured one of these wildmen," he blustered. Previous groups hunted for *yeren* in Shennongjia in 1977, 1980 and 1982. This time, against the better judgment of the expedition scientists and local government officials who feared a stampede of bounty hunters, the China Travel Service in Hubei offered cooking utensils, oil, and grain to wildman hunters and various prizes: 500,000 yuan ($55,000) for bringing one in alive, $5,500 for a dead specimen, up to $4,400 for photographs or video recordings and $1,100 for hair or feces.

On July 11, Xinhua (the New China News Agency) announced that most of the expedition members had returned to Beijing. Wang Fangchen, leader of the 30-member team, said that although the expedition—which used night-vision scopes and satellite orientation gear—ended without any "important findings," some "slim scientific evidence" had been obtained, including possible hair samples. Another search was planned for September.

MALAYSIA'S BIGFOOT

A hunt began in January for *kaki besar,* the Malaysian "Bigfoot," said to be eight feet tall. Army and police units, wildlife experts and local tribesmen combed several thousand square miles of dense jungle surrounding Tanjung Piai in Johor state, where sightings had recently been reported. On January 12, fresh footprints, 18 inches long and displaying only four toes, were found in dense undergrowth, indicating the beast's hideout was nearby. Tribesmen burned twigs and dried leaves, banged tin cans and gongs, performed ritual dances and kept a 24-hour vigil with spears in attempts to

LOOKING GOOD IN THEM GENES

❦ A cow in Chaco, Argentina, gave birth to a calf with six feet, two tails and six testicles on the Twelfth Night (January 6). Cattle rancher Julio Lovey said the prodigy was walking on four of its six legs while the remaining two dangled from its haunches.

❦ Workers building a school near Beijing found more than 300 three-legged frogs living in a pit, said the Xinhua news agency. (Three-legged toads are a Chinese symbol of good luck.)

❦ A one-month-old, two-headed grass snake was discovered on September 15 by Les Paine in a compost heap in Winchelsea, Sussex, England. It was named Foureyes and transferred to the Living World Center in Seaford, Sussex. It seemed to be thriving and was expected to grow to the full three-foot length, provided there were no complications at skin-shedding time. The skin might get tangled up in one of the heads.

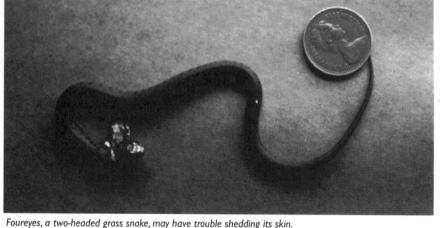

Foureyes, a two-headed grass snake, may have trouble shedding its skin.

drive away the creature, which they said had been sent to Malaysia by evil forces. No follow-up reports have been seen.

....

SUMATRA'S
SHY APEMAN

....

In Sumatra, just across the Malacca Strait from the Malay peninsula, there is an ancient tradition of apelike men in the forests. They are known as *orang pendek* ("little man") or *orang letjo* ("gibbering man"). Orang merely means "man" or "manlike creature"—as in orang utan ("man of the woods"). Orang utang—a frequent misspelling—means "man in debt"! A 1916 *orang pendek* sighting was written up by Dr. Edward Jacobson in a Dutch scientific journal and there have been many sightings since. The creature is a very shy biped, between three and five feet tall, speaking an unintelligible language. It is covered with short dark brown to black hair and has no visible tail. Its arms are not as long as those of an anthropoid ape. It hardly ever climbs trees, but walks on the ground.

Hard evidence of *orang pendek*'s existence might be gathered quite soon. In November 1993, Debbie Martyr, 38, former editor of a south London newspaper, recorded dozens of remarkably consistent eyewitness accounts of the ape-man in and near the jungle-clad mountain in Kerinci Sadlat national park, western Sumatra. Martyr herself saw the creature three times. "He is wonderfully camouflaged," she said. "If he freezes, you can't see him." She brought plaster casts of footprints back to England and on March 6 this year returned to Sumatra with a grant from the Flora and Fauna Preservation Society. She hopes to glean photographic evidence, hair and fecal samples.

PAKISTAN'S BIG HAIRY ONE

Three researchers, two from France and one from Spain, were hunting for the Barmanu ("big hairy one" in local dialect) in the northern mountain region of Chitral in Pakistan last year, part of a long-term project. Trainee zoologist Jordi Magraner had been on the trail for two years. "I've heard its cry twice," he said. "It's a guttural sound, short loud cries which echoed throughout the valley. They reminded you of a human cry and the sound of jackals."

The creature is described as squat and plump with a foul body odor, a large flat nose, protruding eyebrows, a massive neck and a receding forehead. It has large, human-type feet, turned inward, moves with the agility of a goat and is reputedly omnivorous.

MYSTERY FOOTPRINTS IN BORNEO

In 1969, John MacKinnon came upon enigmatic man-like footprints in the remote Ulu Segama national park in Sabah province, northern Borneo. The local name for this "Bigfoot" is batatut. "The toes looked quite human," he wrote, "as did the shapely heel, but the sole was both too short and too broad to be that of a man and the big toe was on the opposite side to what seemed to be the arch of the foot...The size [of the tracks] would be about right for the Asiatic black bear, but the only bear known in Borneo, and peninsular Malaya for that matter, is the Malay sun bear, which is quite small." MacKinnon has discovered three new mammal species on the Vietnam-Laos border since 1992.

WATER MONSTERS

MORGAWR IS BACK

Morgawr is Cornish for "Sea Giant." This renowned monster was seen again off Rosemullion Head in early September by Gertrude Stevens of Golden Bank, England. It was no more than 60 yards away; most of it was below the surface, but Gertrude clearly saw a small head on a long neck, pointing in the direction of Falmouth. The head moved up and down. The creature was at least 20 feet long, with a conical body narrowing towards the tail and a dark yellowish green. "The tail was broad and flat," she said, "like a flat pear shape. I watched it for at least a minute, then it sank down, tail first, very quickly."

Sheila Bird, an author who lives in Falmouth, was delighted to hear of the latest sighting. She saw Morgawr at a distance of 200 yards while walking with her scientist brother, Dr. Eric Bird, off Porthscatho on the evening of July 10. The sea was very calm and it sailed towards them, scarcely making a ripple. "It was about 20 feet long," she said, "with slender neck and small head, moving in a swan-like manner, with head held high." It had a long muscular tail visible just below the surface. They watched the creature for several minutes before it submerged. She said it didn't dive, but dropped vertically without leaving a ripple.

Carrie Ham, 86, of Helford Passage, had a sighting that same year. Looking out her window, she spotted what she took to be an overturned boat in the Helford River. Suddenly what looked like a long arm shaking something shot out of the water. It was the head and neck.

One of the most celebrated sightings was by Falmouth fisherman George Vinnicombe in 1976. He spotted what he also thought was an upturned boat about 30 miles off the Lizard before he, too, saw the head and neck. The last sighting was in 1992; Sheila Bird believes the monster was attracted back to Cornish waters by the hot summer.

Another visitor to Cornish waters in September was a sailfin dory, commonly found off South and West Africa, but thought never to have been seen before near Britain.

MEGA-BEAVER ON THE LOOSE

Since January 1994, a five-foot-long, 80-pound beaver has been gnawing its way through marina docks and birch trees on the Mississippi River at Moline, Illinois. The monster has chewed $1,000 in damage at Marquis Harbor Yacht Club. It has escaped from traps twice and only a blurred photograph exists, prompting the epithet "Nessie." Some people doubt the beaver's existence. "Yeah, right. The beaver that ate Moline," quipped visitor William Morris. The maximum recorded growth for beavers until now is four feet long and 60 pounds.

TEGGIE AND OTHER BEASTS OF BALA

Early last March, brothers Andrew and Paul Delaney from London were fishing on Lake Bala in Gwynedd, North Wales.

"It was very calm and we were about to finish when we noticed something coming up to the surface about 80 yards from the boat. At first we thought it was a tree trunk. Then it straightened up and towered 10 feet in the air. It had a small head and a long neck, like pictures of the Loch Ness Monster."

The first recorded sighting of Lake Bala's monster—nicknamed "Teggie" after Llyn Tegid, the local name for the lake—was made 20 years ago by the former lake warden, Dafydd Bowen. Others have since claimed to have seen a strange shape lurking in the depths of the lake, which is four miles long and 150 feet deep. "I looked out of my office window and saw this thing moving through the water 200 yards away," said Mr. Bowen, now 72, a teetotaler who worked on the lake for 25 years. "It was grey, about eight feet long and looked like a crocodile with a small hump in the middle. Many others have seen it, but most of them are too shy to report their sightings in case they are made fun of."

Dr. Rick Leah, a zoologist at Liverpool University, said in April 1994 that the environmental and evolutionary biology department was keen to use its latest $15,000 digital echo sounder equipment on the lake to look for Teggie, but would need financial backing for the tests.

THE CONGLETON "CROC"

Unnamed visitors to an old quarry used for water sports near Congleton, Cheshire, England, reported sighting a mystery reptile, about three feet long and with a lizard-like head. John Evans, the owner of the center, which is also a wildlife reserve, attempted to catch it, but he did not believe it was a croc. "If it was," he said, "the cold water would soon kill it."

Official opinion concurred. The senior reptile keeper at Chester Zoo suggested that the creature could be a grass snake, adder or a slow-worm while the

owner of the West Midlands Safari Park suggested a lizard. Local speculation favored the notion that a pet crocodile had been released when it had grown too big.

Suggestions that the monster might be a pike received an early setback when quarry anglers reported finding a pike with its sides ripped open. There is some ambiguity here and one has to wonder whether angling gossip about what might have ripped a pike set off the croc scare in the first place.

There has been a storm of media interest in the water park and its new "Do not feed the croc" signs. It would be premature to write the story off, as there are many instances of large reptiles surviving in the British countryside. Of crocs, in particular, a five-footer was found dead in Caerphilly and there were sightings in the River Ouse in 1970 and in the River Stour in Kent in 1975. Charles Fort discovered a report of the capture of a young croc at Over Norton in Oxfordshire in 1836.

LOVESICK GROUPER

The mysterious, intermittent staccato pulses heard in the Pacific near Carmel, California, might be coming from a huge grouper fish, as big as a cow, conjectured Khosrow Lashkari, an acoustics expert at the Monterey Bay Aquarium Research Institute.

"From what I've heard, the males make sounds like this to attract females during the mating season; and apparently this is the mating season," he said. The problem is that the grouper in question prefers warmer climes and had not been reported north of Catalina Island. "But I am told that the waters are warmer than usual here this year," he said. "Perhaps it's a single fish that came too far north and is calling for females."

PACIFIC MONSTER SIGHTED

Gerald Farley sighted what might have been the sea monster Cadborosaurus off Canada's Pacific coast from his flat in Douglas Street, James Bay, on September 28 last year.

Spotted at 1:50 P.M., the object was black, snake-like and 30 feet long. There were no humps or sign of a head. It was up for about a minute and Farley watched it through binoculars. There were no boats and no waves. This was the first Caddy sighting since the spring; there have been more than 50 years of sightings.

THE
NATURAL
WORLD

THE NATURAL WORLD

This is where we look at the plate-tectonics of weirdness—planet-scale abnormality. From plagues to meteors, earthquakes to falling fish, volcanic eruptions to vast snowfalls, it's in here.

Most noticeable this year was the continuing slump in crop circles—there were too few, in fact, to warrant a category. Perhaps this is connected with 1995's stunning heat wave—lots of witnesses about in the fields late at night, and less opportunity to get into mischief. The heat wave also contributed to the increase in Meteorological Superlatives. Epidemics were up, thanks to the Ebola virus scare, and a balloon in astrological activity required a new category: Cosmological Superlatives. All this was balanced by a fall in other areas, leaving the Natural World's Strangeness Index value at the same earth-shaking 1994 level.

DISASTERS, NATURAL & MAN-MADE

BARBECUED BACON IN HAMM

A truckload of sausages and bacon sizzled to a crisp after the truck's brakes caught fire in Hamm, Germany. Meanwhile, motorists in England found themselves in a jam—literally. The northbound highway near Warrington was reduced to one lane after a truck shed its load of 40 tons of jam.

LIME-BASTED

A farmer's shed was destroyed by fire on the Japanese island of Shikoku in June 1994. The skeletons of two kittens and a package of quicklime were found lying in the ashes. Since lime is flammable when wet, it was thought that the fire was started by the kittens peeing on the bag of lime.

PARATROOPING REDBACKS

Drought and high winds caused a plague of redback spiders in Brisbane, Australia, and the surrounding Queensland countryside on September 24. The spiders, with their potentially lethal bite, parachuted in on their silk webs.

DROUGHT, FIRE AND HAZE

Six months of drought were followed by fires covering 247,000 acres of tropical rainforest on Sumatra and in Kalimantan, Indonesia, in October, the worst since 1982. Haze spread over much of Malaysia and Singapore, hampering air and sea traffic and possibly causing the collision between two vessels off Riau province, between Sumatra and Singapore. Huge coal and peat deposits helped to fuel the fires.

TODDLER FLOATS IN FIERY FLOOD

At least 506 people died in the Egyptian town of Dronka (or Durunka), 250 miles upriver from Cairo, when a railway bridge over an army fuel depot collapsed during torrential rain (the worst in 50 years) on November 2. According to some reports, the fuel tanks were struck by lightning. Pipelines were ruptured and about 15,000 tons of burning fuel on top of floodwaters roared through the town. It took 10 hours to control the blaze. "When we tried to put out the flames with the water the fire just grew bigger," said one witness. "It was like hell." More than 200 buildings were destroyed and many more were completely blackened up to the third floor. Elsewhere in Egypt, 94 people were stung by scorpions floating on the floodwaters.

Three days later, farmer Abdel Hamdan Yuner was trying to drain the water from his flooded field nine miles outside Dronka when he found a seven-month-old boy in good health, floating like Moses on straw bedding. The farmer drove around on his tractor, announcing the news through a loudspeaker. An aunt claimed the child, Hussein Tolba el-Hattab, whose parents and seven brothers and sisters were presumed dead in Dronka.

BIOLOGICAL AND MEDICAL

MISASSEMBLED MAN

An inquest in Southwark, London, was told that a fit man of 24 was found to have his stomach, pancreas, colon and spleen in his left chest rather than his abdomen. He died unexpectedly in June.

COMMANDO GETS "MIRACLE" HAND RELIEF IN THE JUNGLE

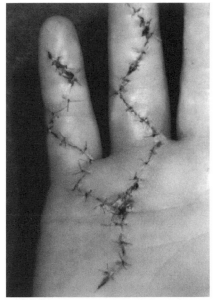

Sergeant Mann's gangrenous hand after being cured by a medicine woman's snake flesh stew.

Sergeant Bob Mann, a Territorial army commando from Plymouth, England, was part of the 10-man team that became lost in Low's Gully, Borneo, while attempting to navigate Mount Kinabalu in March 1994.

The group split into three parties, with Sgt. Mann and Lt. Cpl. Richard Mayfield attempting to find their own way out of the jungle. Three days later, Sgt. Mann slipped and fell on his machete, almost severing two fingers on his right hand and cutting his palm through to the bone. Despite treating the wound with iodine, it soon became gangrenous and smelled like rotting meat. Sgt. Mann was convinced that he would lose his fingers or even his hand. After eight days, the two men found their way out of the jungle and walked into the small village of Kampung Melangkap Kapa, where Sgt. Mann collapsed.

A village elder summoned a "medicine woman," who thrust the gangrenous hand into a jar containing snake's flesh, wild herbs and ground animal bones. "I was too weak to argue," said Sgt. Mann. "It felt as though my hand was on fire and when she pulled it out about 20 minutes later the skin was spotlessly clean. It was unbelievable. The pus had gone and the open wound had been fused."

Sgt. Mann was flown to the British Military Hospital in Hong Kong, where he had an operation on the tendons, leaving him with more than 40 stitches, and faced two more operations to replace damaged tissue. He was told that the medicine woman had saved his

PECULIAR PRESS

ICEBERG BLAMED FOR DYSENTERY
South Devon Herald Express,
July 26, 1994

ANTS SHOW BRITISH TRANSIT HOW TO CONTROL COMPUTERS
Daily Telegraph, July 21, 1994

ALADDIN'S CAVE WINS VILLAGE SHOP AWARD
The Times (London),
July 22, 1994

hand. The Royal Army Medical Corps was eager to contact her to find out what was in the potion and assimilate an apparent miracle into Western medicine.

SUMMER'S BASTARD

Judy Blaby, 68, from Tamworth, England, has found an apple growing on her clematis, which stands a yard away from an apple tree. "It's definitely an apple," she said, "although it's green and the fruit on the nearby tree is red." Experts were incredulous.

JURASSIC BARK

Last August, David Noble, an officer of Australia's National Parks and Wildlife Service, descended into a 1,800-foot gorge after walking for several hours through almost impenetrable bush and discovered a genus of tree thought to have died out 150 million years ago.

Botanist Ken Hill compares newly discovered foliage with fossils dating back 150 million years.

The find was made in Wollemi National Park, about 125 miles west of Sydney in the Blue Mountains of New South Wales. Named the Wollemi Pine, the biggest is 130 feet high with a 10-foot girth, indicating a minimum age of 150 years. Only 23 adult trees and 16 juveniles have been found so far,

making it one of the world's rarest plants. They are covered in dense, waxy foliage and have a distinctive bark that makes them appear to be coated in bubbly brown chocolate. "Wollemi" is an aboriginal word meaning "look around you," which is just how Noble found the prehistoric pines. One of the 40 Wollemi Pine seeds collected from the 1.2-acre grove sprouted in Mount Annan Botanic Garden on December 15, 1994.

"This is a plant family that was widespread, including the Northern Hemisphere, before the great extinction …when we lost the dinosaurs. It links the history of our flora to a time before Australia was a continent of its own," said Dr. Barbara Briggs, scientific director of Sydney's Royal Botanic Gardens.

Dr. Briggs compared the discovery to that of other living fossils such as the dawn redwood tree in China in 1944 and the coelacanth fish in 1938 off Madagascar.

TREES GROOVE TO RADIO WAVES

Nine years ago, the U.S. Navy installed a 60-mile wire antenna in a Michigan forest to communicate with submarines using extremely low frequency (76 Hertz) radio waves. "Project ELF" started operating at low power in 1986, moving to full power three years later. Forestry researchers have now discovered that the trunks of nearby aspen and red maple trees have grown 50 percent thicker than on a control site 30 miles away, while red pines have grown 10 percent taller.

Northern red oak and paper birch, however, appear to be unaffected. Glenn Mroz of the Michigan Technological University in Houghton said that the study was not intended to find what caused the spurt in growth, but laboratory experiments suggested that the electromagnetic field might accelerate the transport of nutrients such as calcium across cell walls.

SYDNEY TEENAGER TURNS INTO RADIO

A 17-year-old youth who climbed a broadcasting mast in Sydney, Australia, was severely burned and rattled "like a radio speaker." A massive flow of about 50 kW of radio frequency current passed through his body to the ground. Friends who had accompanied him described the current arcing between his hand and the mast, causing sound waves and making him wow and hum like a badly tuned radio. They took him to Liverpool Hospital in southwest Sydney, where he spent four days under observation while being treated with morphine for severe pain.

Telecom Australia's chief medical officer, Bruce Hocking, and two consultants from Liverpool Hospital, who wrote up the accident in the *Medical Journal of Australia,* said incidents of radio frequency electric shock and burns were so rare that they knew of only one other case of comparable severity. The VHF current did not act directly on cell membranes, but stimulated nerves, causing extreme pain. The team warned that possible side effects included heart irregularities, cataracts and the reversible loss of sperm.

SEE YOU IN 95, BRO

Celeste Keys was born in Ochsner Foundation Hospital, New Orleans, on January 18, 95 days after her twin brother Timothy. The delay beat the old record of 56 days set in 1953 by a woman with a double uterus (the record for delayed triplets, 45 days, was set in 1993). The mother, schoolteacher Simone Keys, had high blood pressure,

a heart rhythm irregularity and childhood rheumatic fever. Doctors wanted to prevent a premature birth, but she went into labor on October 11 and they were able to delay Timothy's birth by only four days. He was 15 weeks premature and weighed just 1 pound, 14 ounces. He is at risk for neurological problems such as mild cerebral palsy.

Drugs quieted Keys' contractions and the delivery table was upended so that her head was pointing to the floor. The umbilical cord was trimmed as close as possible to the mouth of the womb, after which the cervix was stitched up. Keys went home in early November, while Timothy stayed in hospital. Celeste was born vaginally at full term, weighing 5 pounds, 15 ounces, 13 ounces more than her three-month-old twin.

MULTI-ETHNIC FAMILY

Ms. Marian Walsh, 30, gave birth to twins Louise and Reece in May in the Whittington Hospital, north London. Reece is black, his sister is white. Ms. Walsh's partner, Curtis Simmons, is West Indian and black. The couple, from Tottenham, expected the twins to be mid-brown like Marian's nine-year-old son, Luke. The twins developed from separate eggs, but it is unusual to see such a striking contrast in skin tone.

DOUBLE-WOMBED WONDERGIRLS

Cynthia Silveira, who has two wombs, delivered a healthy, premature baby girl in San Jose, California, on October 10, 1994, eight days after giving birth to Hope, the girl's twin, from the other womb. Doctors expected to deliver the baby by Cesarean section because she was conceived in a "blind" uterus with

UNCOMBABLE HAIR SYNDROME

For some people that old excuse "I've just washed my hair and I can't do a thing with it" takes on sinister significance: they are the unfortunate victims of a rare affliction, Hair Felting or Uncombable Hair Syndrome.

The first known case was reported in 1884 by a British doctor named LePage. His patient was a 17-year-old girl whose hair had become a hard tangled lump on the right side of her head after being washed. LePage decided she had hysterical tendencies, explaining that "high nervous tension…found vent in the hair itself." He named the affliction *Plica neuropathica*—and for him, at least, the problem was solved.

Further cases around the same time were reported by other medical practitioners. The hair of an Indian woman had formed a hard and firm elongated mass on the back of her head, and was described as rope-like and about fist-size. In another case, the *Plica* occupied a coin-size area above the nape of the neck and in 12 years apparently grew to a length of 12 feet. Ten or so further cases turned up between LePage's time and the 1950s. Virtually all were written off as the result of hysteria, the fashionable catch-all explanation at the time for anything the medical profession didn't understand affecting women—much as archeologists use "ritual object" to cover any artifact they can't account for. Surely, most people would become a touch hysterical if their hair suddenly went solid.

At least two subsequent cases have occurred. One was reported in the August 1993 issue of *Archives of Dermatology* and concerned a woman of 39 whose hair suddenly fell out and was replaced by dry, coarse curly hair which was so tangled it was impossible to comb. It lacked knots, kinks or twists which would explain the tangling, but the hairs themselves were strangely shaped, the cross-sections being triangular, grooved, or like kidney beans.

The researchers at the Cleveland Clinic Foundation in Ohio where the victim was treated were unable to explain the phenomenon, but in a case reported in Judith Stone's *How to Tell a Crouton from a Proton* (1991), Indiana University's Dermatology Clinic believed it had the answer. Their victim was a 40-year-old woman with waist-length hair, a monstrous gnarled mass which Stone graphically describes as "looking like a cross between a tornado and Bigfoot."

Dermatologists Julia Marshall and Colleen Parker investigated and came to the conclusion that the problems were mechanical, a result of the hair surface being made up of overlapping scales. As the hair gets older, the scales become more vulnerable to being flipped up, which makes them more likely to be damaged. If hair in this condition is vigorously scrubbed when wet, the scales which have flipped up can interdigitate, locking together and turning the hair into a solid, uncombable mass. This is exactly how wool is treated to turn it into felt; the wool is teased out into individual fibers, soaked and then agitated until it becomes a tightly matted mass—hence the term *hair felting*, coined in 1970. All the reported cases are in women, probably because few men grow their hair long enough for cuticular interdigitation to take place. Usually, the solution is to cut the mass of solidified hair off, but in the Indiana case, the woman wanted to keep it if at all possible, having spent 24 years growing it. After two-and-a-half months of lubricating with olive oil and separating it with knitting needles, her hair returned to normal.

no opening for a baby to get out; but the wall separating the two wombs ruptured during contractions, allowing Hailey Silveira to slide out through the first uterus. "Nature wrote its own book," said the relieved father.

URINE LUCK!

Morarji Desai, the world's oldest head of government when he was prime minister of India between 1977 and 1979, died in Bombay on April 10 at the age of 99. A strong proponent of teetotalism and yoga, he attributed his longevity to drinking his urine—which he called "the water of life"—at least twice a day since he was 61. "I have seen cases of diabetes, cancer and tuberculosis cured by it," he said. "For diseases of the eyes, ears, teeth and skin it is the most effective remedy." In 1978 he defended pee drinking on American television: "In America now you are preparing extracts from it for heart trouble," he told viewers. "So you drink other people's urine, but not your own." He ate two meals a day consisting of milk, fruit juice, vegetables and garlic.

Former Indian Prime Minister Morarji Desai loved a daily drop of his own.

As it turns out, recent medical reports on the health benefits of melatonin have sent Americans flocking to drug stores in search of supplemental tablets. But urine is rich in melatonin, a hormone which can act as a modest pain killer or soporific. Released by the pineal gland overnight, its production is shut off by light shining in the eyes. It plays some unknown role in setting our various daily (circadian) rhythms and may be part of the body's "master clock." Handy travelers' tip: a nice warm cup of pee at bedtime seems to lessen the trauma of jet lag.

Urine drinking is also widespread among Indian yogis, who call it amaroli. Taking melatonin upon waking may convince the body that it has had more sleep, useful for yogis who start meditating at an ungodly hour in the morning. It might also slow down brain-wave activity, enhancing meditation, and reduce the pain of sitting absolutely still for hours. Melatonin must be taken regularly to reset sleep cycles; the traditional yogic texts urge that "auto-urine" be taken daily for a month. Many yogis maintain that the urine of prepubescent children is more effective than their own.

Pee-drinking is on the rise in Britain, the most famous exponent being the actress Sarah Miles. Simon Kirby, of the Immune Deficiency Trust (a holistic medical center in London) says several people with AIDS-related illnesses are doing it. "It undoubtedly makes them feel better," he said. Keith Slocombe, 64, started drinking his own water over 30 years ago when recovering from a liver disorder. "I've known hundreds of people to benefit from it over the years," he said. "One woman was so grateful for the pain relief it gave her she would drink it at parties instead of champagne."

J.W. Armstrong's 1944 treatise *The Water of Life* is regarded by connoisseurs as definitive. He was inspired by a quirky interpretation of Proverbs 5:15: "Drink waters out of thine own cistern." He claimed to have cured himself of TB within six weeks and maintained that the practice was useful in the treat-

THE SCHWASCAR AWARDS

FREE-FALL FIASCO

❦ On September 3, 1994, Sharon McClelland, 26, was making her second parachute jump—her first free fall—near Queensville, Ontario, when her chute only partially opened. "She failed to follow proper procedure and open her backup chute," said Frank Watts, owner of the parachute school. She plummeted 10,000 feet, landing on her back in a marsh. Almost at once, she got up and apologized to her skydiving instructor. "It's the strangest reaction I've ever seen," he said. She was uninjured, apart from some bruising.

RUNNERS-UP

❦ A DC-9 airliner blew up 10 miles from the Colombian city of Cartegena on January 11 and the wreckage fell 14,000 feet into a swamp. All 52 passengers and crew were killed, with the sole exception of nine-year-old Erika Delgado, who was thrown out of the burning plane by her mother, and landed on a thick cushion of water lilies. She escaped with broken arms, a broken leg and an abdominal injury. Two farmers stole her gold necklace before others rescued her and took her to a neighboring village. She was discharged from the hospital in Cartegena on January 22.

❦ Des Maloney, 28, was catapulted from the cockpit of a Provost jet as his elder brother flew upside down at 250 mph. The ejector seat had fired accidentally at 3,000 feet, hurling him through the plastic canopy. Describing how he spun to earth in a parachute that failed to open properly before beginning to strangle him, he said: "It was a bit of a shock. I knew I was in big trouble when I wasn't in the airplane any more." He landed in a field outside a supermarket near Colchester, England. The first person on the scene was a 14-year-old boy who asked him for his parachute. Des suffered no serious injuries and spent one day in the hospital. His brother, Tom, managed to maintain control of the 25-year-old plane and land it safely at North Weald Airport, 20 miles away. The ejector seat hit the roof of a house in nearby Stanway and made its own landing outside the front door.

❦ Skydiver John Goodyear, of the Black Knights team, was the first to leap from an aircraft on June 25, 1994, during a school fete in Preston, England. His main parachute got entangled with the emergency chute and he plummeted 3,000 feet. His landing was broken by a tree and he was found hanging 20 feet from the ground. He was treated in the hospital for a broken leg and minor injuries.

❦ The following month, Bill Coomber plunged 4,500 feet above Headcorn ærodrome in Kent, England, when both his main and emergency chutes became entangled. He managed to throw his emergency chute clear, allowing his main chute to open 200 feet from the ground. He suffered back injuries, but was able to walk away.

ment of gangrene, cancer, leukemia and heart disease. Charles Wansborough, a modern disciple of Armstrong's, believes urine therapy allows the body to cure itself, a process he calls "isopathy." His theory is that urine is a convenient and cheap source of valuable mineral salts such as creatine, sodium and potassium. It also contains an enzyme, urokinase, effective in countering blood clotting.

Urine-drinking has caught on in Taiwan in a big way, where an estimated 200,000 people do it to cure disease, improve health and achieve longevity. Their mentor, Chen Ching-chuan, 65, drinks three cups a day and passes for a man 20 years younger. In 1992, a lay Buddhist in the country published *The Magic Golden Water Cure,* documenting putative dramatic pee-tippling cures for serious illnesses.

WHY WOMEN WOO WHOPPERS

While women make up less than two percent of Britain's 4.5 million anglers, they nevertheless hold all the big catch records for the king of fish—the salmon.

Georgina Ballantine holds the rod and line record with a 64-pound catch in the Tay in 1922; Clementine Morrison has the fly fishing record with a 61-pound catch in the Deveron in 1924; Doreen Davey took the spring run record with a 59-pound catch in the Wye in 1922; and Gladys Huntingdon is still the holder of the West Coast catch record with a 55-pound catch in the Awe in 1927.

Peter Behan, a neurological scientist at Glasgow University, in his recently-published book *Salmon and Women: The Feminine Angle*, claims that female angling success is spurred by a pheromone which is emitted through the woman's skin and urine. This is particularly attractive to male salmon, which are

larger than the females. According to Irish folklore, anglers should tie lures with wool from a young girl's clothes if they want a big catch.

Dr. Dick Shelton, head of the fisheries laboratory at Pitlochry, is slightly disappointed that his own team's research hasn't found anything to support the female scent theory. "As grilse [young salmon] are largely male, you would expect female anglers to catch large numbers of them on the rivers Tay and Dee, where they are abundant," he said. "This doesn't seem to happen." However, women keep landing the whoppers.

FOREVER AMBER

Microbes from a stingless bee entombed in amber for up to 40 million years have been revived at the California Polytechnic State University in San Luis Obispo. Raul Cano and Monica Borucki announced their results in May, although even before publication skeptical scientists were labeling the claim implausible and suggesting it was the result of accidental contamination of the laboratory specimens.

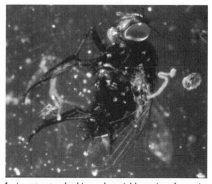

An insect entombed in amber yields ancient bacteria.

The bee came from amber collected in the Dominican Republic, in the West Indies. Cano split the amber and dissected the bee, obtaining microbial spores from the insect's gut. After a couple of weeks in a growth medium, the spores began to reproduce. Cano identified the bacteria as similar to the *Bacillus sphericus* found in modern bees, both by their shape and from the sequence of their ribosomal DNA.

In what sounds like a good answer to the critics, he's able to state that the material is similar to modern material, but with differences, probably explained by mutations that have occurred since the bee was entombed.

Bacteria form spores by coating themselves in layers of protein when conditions turn nasty, and such spore-survivals are already known over periods of thousands of years. Cano hopes to be able to discover new chemicals in the material, which might lead to the development of new antibiotics.

····························

HUM MISTY FOR ME

····························

Vets at the Animal Health Trust in Newmarket, England, had just removed a tumor from the lip of a five-year-old Welsh pony called Misty when they heard a high-pitched noise, a bit like feedback from an amplifier, coming from its right ear. The pony, described in the April issue of the *Veterinary Record,* seemed oblivious to the sound, although it could be heard three feet away. It varied in intensity, but stayed at a constant pitch of 7 kiloHertz. Misty's owners had been aware of the noise for about three years.

Tinnitus—the sound of ringing in the ears—is familiar to anyone who has heard an explosion or listened to very loud music. The sensation usually wears off, although some people "hear" a constant ringing which disrupts concentration and can cause chronic health problems. This is called "subjective tinnitus." Much rarer is when other people hear the noise, a condition called "objective tinnitus."

Joe Mayhew, head of the veterinary team, suggested that the nerve cells in the ear were firing spontaneously, causing the hair cells to vibrate and make the ossicles and the eardrum resonate. Ellis Douek, an ear, nose and throat surgeon at Guy's Hospital in London, disagrees. Spontaneous nerve activity can cause sounds, he says, but these cannot be heard without powerful microphones. Audible sounds are "very rare indeed" and are usually caused by spasms in the muscles of the inner ear or throat, or by resonance due to abnormalities in the ear's blood supply.

Mayhew said that it was impossible to tell whether animals experience the same sensations as tinnitus sufferers, although it could explain why some horses repeatedly shake their heads for no obvious reason.

According to Professor Ian Russell of Sussex University, a couple in Leicestershire called an engineer to repair their TV set before discovering that the whining sound in the room was coming from their child's ears.

EPIDEMICS AND ILLNESS

BUBONIC PLAGUE PLOT FOILED

Larry Harris, 43, a white supremacist from Lancaster, Ohio, was arrested on May 12 for procuring $300 worth of *Yersinia pesatis,* the bacteria that causes bubonic plague, from a biomedical supply company in Rockville, Maryland, by falsely claiming he owned a laboratory. Until he was fired on May 15, he was a well and tank inspector with a company called Superior Labs, where he was qualified only to test drinking water for bacteria.

Police searching Harris's home found a document certifying him as a member of the Church of Jesus Christ Christian Aryan Nations, hand grenade triggers, homemade explosive devices and detonating fuses. They confiscated the freeze-dried bacteria—harmless in that form—before Harris could reconstitute it, using heat and water.

He pleaded not guilty to receiving stolen property for obtaining the bacteria by fraud, which carries a maximum penalty of 18 months in jail and a $2,500 fine. Harris had told a health official that he needed the bacteria to conduct "biomedical research using rats to counteract imminent invasion from Iraq of super germ-carrying rats." Bubonic plague carried off up to one third of the European population in the 14th century.

FREAKISH FERTILIZER

Frank Kulczynski, 76, collapsed in his garden in McKeesport, near Pittsburgh, on April 25, 1994. His son said he had been fertilizing his lawn. Two hospital workers developed rashes when they

LOVE HURTS

❤ Hans Meyer, 35, spread a blanket in the trunk of his BMW and climbed in with a female companion in May 1994. During their lovemaking the trunk slammed shut, locking them in. Fortunately, Meyer had his mobile phone with him and managed to call the police at Erlenback, Germany. They eventually freed the pair, but only after being persuaded that the phone call was not a joke.

❤ An unnamed man in California was fitted with a prototype electronic implant by doctors in 1992. This was designed to help impotent men rise to the occasion by remote control. Unfortunately, the 52-year-old patient got a lift every time his neighbors used their electronic car doors.

❤ A drunken night of passion came to a climax in July 1990 when a brunette allowed her boyfriend to paint her from head to toe in yacht varnish. The finishing touch was added when he made her wear a dog collar as well. The trouble began the next morning, when she tried to scrub off her gloss finish. Unable to remove it and still wearing the dog collar, she headed off to her local hospital in Gillingham, England, in search of help. When asked how she had got into the predicament, she turned shy and vanished. Fearing she was a fire risk in that condition, doctors informed the police, who eventually tracked her down and returned her to the hospital, where the varnish was finally removed.

touched him. Others complained of headaches or other ailments. Four were hospitalized overnight for observation and released with no symptoms. The man's skin was hot although he had no fever; his skin was blistering and peeling, and blood poured from his mouth. One reported an ammonia-like odor; another said the patient smelled of chlorine. A possible insect bite was noted on his neck when he was brought in. Kulczynski died in the hospital and a high-security autopsy was planned.

BLEACHY BILLOW

Shortly before 3 P.M. on August 9, 1994, a mysterious cloud descended on Murphy Middle School, just off Santa Teresa Boulevard in San Jose, California, causing a burning feeling in the eyes, throats and chests of 50 children and teachers, who were rushed to local emergency rooms. Some reported a "bleachy" type of smell. The cloud dissipated as rapidly as it had arrived, leaving no residue, odor or physical evidence.

NO ONE'S SINGING IN THIS RAIN

❦ A brown shower landed on spectators at an East of Scotland tournament at Craiglockhart Tennis Club, Colinton, Scotland, in August. John Paterson said: "I was sitting on the grass watching the tennis when I heard a loud slap. I looked around and my wife Jane's back and arms were covered in human excrement. Several other people sitting near her were covered too. The smell was unbearable—no one would go near them." At first, the Edinburgh-to-Birmingham shuttle, which was passing overhead at the time, was blamed; but stringent checks of the aircraft's sewage tanks ruled this out. Edinburgh airport said the shower could not have come from an aircraft. Edinburgh District Council, which confirmed that the feces were human, could offer no alternative explanation and environmental health officers were no nearer a solution more than a month later.

❦ A clear jelly-like substance, cold to the touch, was discovered in a garden in Horley, England, on September 23. The finder, who wants to remain anonymous, said: "I don't know what it is, but if I had scraped it all up, there would have been enough to fill a kettle." A friend, Ian Lawson of Banbury, who was visiting at the time, said: "It has obviously come from the sky. Maybe it is some form of refrigeration substance used on aircraft." No more of the substance was found in neighboring gardens.

❦ Delighted villagers grabbed handfuls of money when £10 notes fluttered out of the sky over Kidlington, England, on February 20, 1995. Police admitted they were baffled by the windfall. At 6 A.M. on March 24, a motorist saw clouds of greenbacks floating across the four-lane McClellan Highway in East Boston, Massachusetts. Police recovered $7,070 in various denomination bills, but had no idea how much was pocketed by the public. By the following morning, no one had called the police station to claim the money.

EBOLA EXPLAINED

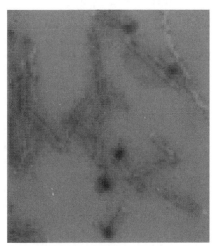

The Ebola virus that sparked world terror and a curious folktale.

Last May there was an outbreak of the Ebola virus in Kikwit, a city of 600,000, 370 miles inland from Kinshasa, the capital of Zaire. It later spread to Mosango, 60 miles from Kikwit, Yassa Bonga, 156 miles away, and possibly to Kenge, only 130 miles east of Kinshasa. The Hollywood film *Outbreak*, starring Dustin Hoffman and based on the 1989 appearance of the less-deadly Ebola Reston virus in a Washington primate quarantine unit, had just been released.

The filovirus (worm-shaped virus) Ebola Zaire was first discovered in 1976, when 274 of 300 people infected died in an outbreak. It is not known where it originated. At first the symptoms are similar to those of flu. A day or two later, blood trickles from the eyes, ears and nose. As the virus multiplies inside the body, it attacks all the organs, which jam with congealed blood and then disintegrate while surrounding tissue bleeds uncontrollably. Delirium and death usually follow within days. There is no antidote. Like the HIV virus, Ebola is thought to have spread to humans from African monkeys. Transmission is, however, easy

to control as it requires direct contact with an infected person or his/her bodily secretions; although there is always the danger that the virus might mutate to spread like a cold.

By May 18, according to the World Health Organization (WHO), the death toll was 79, but figures were hard to determine. Medical sources in Kinshasa announced that the first victim was Kimfumu, 36, a laboratory assistant who, while hunting for diamonds in Angola, contracted the disease from someone who had eaten smoked monkey, and returned to Kikwit on April 9. However, the WHO said the first victim was admitted to Kikwit hospital at the end of March, where he infected Kimfumu. Later, the blame was shifted to the family of a forest worker, seven members of which had died since December.

An odd folktale emerged in connection with the epidemic. Several months earlier, a woman was said to have wandered into Kikwit with a terrible stomachache. A doctor opened up her stomach and discovered two flawless, sparkling diamonds, which he stole, bringing down a curse on himself and everyone who witnessed or benefited from the deed. It was this curse that caused the illness, not the Ebola virus. The diamond tale had many variations, but all started with a diamond thief from Angola swallowing the gems and ended with the curse.

MYSTERY FUMES

Dr. Julie Gorchynski, the main victim in the California fumes case of February 1994, where hospital staff were felled by mysterious ammonia-like fumes allegedly coming from cancer victim Gloria Ramirez, filed a $6 million claim against Riverside Hospital in August.

She had suffered bone necrosis, restrictive lung disease, elevated liver and pancreatic enzymes, gastritis, hepatitis and unexplained crystals in her blood. So far she has had three operations on her knees and will possibly never work again. The Ramirez family have also filed a suit, claiming that the hospital was responsible for the fumes.

On September 2, the California Department of Health Services announced that the fume casualties had been victims of mass hysteria ("mass sociogenic illness"), although it was possible that some staff had been exposed to something inside Ramirez's body, but its significance was unknown; chemists were trying to identify it. Eleven people had reported smelling an unusual odor; after five collapsed and the emergency room was evacuated, 23 people complained of at least one symptom—most commonly headache, dizziness and nausea.

The researchers for the study, Dr. Ana Osorio and Dr. Kirsten Waller, didn't see the raw data of the Ramirez autopsies. Gorchynski said they didn't interview her or review her medical records and that their conclusions were "absurd and ridiculous." She wondered if the cause of the trouble might be ethylene oxide, a toxic gas used to sterilize medical equipment.

FT's suggestion last May, after consulting California police sources, that the fumes might have resulted from the use of DMSO (dimethyl sulphoxide) by Ramirez, did not appear in any other public news report until the Lawrence Livermore National Laboratory report was made public six months later, on November 3. Although it is not prescribed in the United States, DMSO is sold on the black market and can be obtained in Mexico. It is portrayed in the scientific literature as something of a wonder drug for its analgesic and anti-inflammatory properties, and has been used as an anti-bacterial agent in cancer patients and for therapy of cervical cancer—which is what Ramirez had. DMSO cream, which is easily absorbed by the skin, has been used as a carrier to deliver the recreational drug PCP ("angel dust") which, according to California's Occupational Safety and Health Administration's own report on the fumes incident, Ramirez had used.

Although it was not known whether Ramirez had used DMSO, the oily sheen seen on her body by nurse Balderas could be evidence of such use. Furthermore, DMSO is metabolized through oxidation to become dimethyl sulphone, which was found in her system. This had been triggered by the huge amounts of the headache and pain reliever Tylenol in her bloodstream, and a state of dehydration brought about by several days of vomiting. The process was probably accelerated when paramedics administered oxygen as she was rushed to hospital. When blood was drawn from Ramirez in the emergency room, the sharp drop in temperature of her blood—from body temperature to the cool air of the hospital—could have created dimethyl sulphate, a chemical warfare agent, which would account for the crystals in her blood sample. Her body temperature was too high for the deadly compound to be produced internally.

The symptoms displayed by the medical staff were consistent with fleeting exposure to the toxin, which can be lethal in small quantities, but which rapidly dissipates. Lawrence Livermore chemist Patrick Grant admitted that their suggested solution to the mystery had come about through serendipity. "It was lucky that all three compounds that we were dealing with were listed on the same [chemical resource] page," he said.

"There are some emergency room personnel who could be very lucky to be alive," said Riverside County Coroner Scotty Hill, who released the Lawrence Livermore report. He endorsed the findings, quietly dropping the earlier suggestion of mass hysteria. The new official explanation, while considerably more interesting than the earlier ones, remains unproven.

FALLS FROM THE SKY

SAHARAN SANDS RAIN DOWN ON NORTH

Puzzled motorists throughout Northern Ireland reported finding their cars covered in a brown, watery substance on May 2, 1994. The Meteorological Office claimed it was sand from the Sahara blown 2,000 miles by southerly or southeasterly winds. Hillsborough Road gas station in Lisburn said that car wash business was up 50 percent.

The following morning, further sand fell on the Inverness area in Scotland. Met Office forecaster Richard Page of Aberdeen said: "For some reason this happens most often between Inverness and Elgin. It is extremely rare for us to receive enquiries about things like this either from the West Coast or here in the Aberdeen area." He said the sand might come from either the Sahara or the Canary Islands.

FT reader Donald D. Mitchell has sent us a sample of the sand which he collected from the lids of his fish tanks in Duartmore Bridge, Sutherland.

EAU DE PIG SLURRY

"It's one of the worst smells we've had in years," said a spokesman for the Meteorological Office, who acknowledged that a large number of public complaints had been made on the night of April 24. The smell, described as a mixture of rotting eggs, manure and industrial waste, had nostrils twitching all along the coast of Kent, England. The miasma hung over southeastern England—particularly in the coastal parts of Norfolk, Kent, Sussex and Hampshire—and was reported as far inland as Leicestershire and the East Midlands.

British Gas said it received more than 2,000 calls from people fearing a gas main leak.

John Bower, head of air monitoring at the AEA National Environment Technology Centre in Culham, Oxfordshire (where, oddly, nothing could be smelled officially), said it was a difficult riddle to solve because of "an unusual weather system" currently over southern England which had been over the German-Dutch border the previous day, and over Poland before that. The typically British reaction to nasty smells—"It's not me!"—deferred blame to foreigners: the pig farms of Denmark and Holland and pollution-belching factories of Rotterdam, the Ruhr and Poland.

Peter Cresswell, a Met Office forecaster in Southampton, said the last time a smell of this magnitude happened was "about seven years ago" and was also blamed on Dutch pig farmers, who keep vast quantities of effluent in huge slurry ponds. "The smell sits close to the ground and light winds bring it over here," said Mr. Cresswell. Bower, however, was more cautious: "If it was coming from a single point source it would be very unlikely to affect such a large area."

By noon the following day, the odor or "pong" had been wafted away by northerly breezes from Scandinavia. Curious thing: surely "light winds" have wafted to these shores from Holland at times other than "seven years ago," so why did these not carry the tang of pig slurry? If, at other times, the winds blow elsewhere, do the folk in other countries downwind complain? *FT* has no obvious notes of this. In fact Paul van der Berg of the ministry responsible for the environment in the Hague rejected the English explanation: "It's just not possible," he insisted. "If you could smell it over in England, think how bad the air would be here,

but it's not at all." The Belgian agricultural minister, too, denied national responsibility.

The mystery remains: where did the "Euro-pong" (as the tabloids dubbed it) come from? Could there be any possible connection to "an obnoxious smell" that revolted the residents of the Stratton district of Swindon in Euro-pong-free Oxfordshire, reported earlier the same month? The details are different, however; here the smell is likened to cat piss. It stings skin and eyes, causes fits of coughing and has been noticed intermittently for more than a year, defying attempts by Thamesdown environmental officers to trace its source.

SPONTANEOUS HUMAN COMBUSTION

COFFIN LIGHTS UP DURING FUNERAL

On the evening of June 1, 1994, minutes after the departure of mourners from the funeral of Wycliff Robertson—a 25-year-old victim of a shooting—at Mount Gillian Baptist Church in Baton Rouge, Louisiana, undertakers found smoke pouring from the closed coffin.

Morticians from Winnfield Funeral Home were called to the church earlier

in the evening to work on the dead man, following complaints of an odor coming from the casket.

"We believe that whatever chemical was added that second time caused the reaction that started the fire beside the body," said arson investigator Haley Carter. The body was not badly burned and Robertson was buried in a new coffin two days later. Thousands of bodies are embalmed worldwide, so we must ask why this phenomenon is not more frequent.

ARCHIVE GEMS

JELLYFISH LINKED TO FALL OF GOO

On August 7, 1994, small blobs of clear, gelatinous goo fell with rain on and around the house in Oakville, Washington, which Sunny Barclift shares with her mother, Dotty Hearn, on a 29-acre farm in Grays Harbor County. The blobs, about half the size of rice grains, might have gone unnoticed if some had not landed on the black asphalt-covered roof of a small shed.

Barclift had moved to Oakville last year from Phoenix where she had been director of occupational safety and health for the Arizona branch of the National Safety Council. Following the blob fall, Hearn went to the hospital suffering from dizziness and nausea. Barclift and a friend also had minor bouts of nausea and fatigue after collecting and touching the mysterious gloop. A newly adopted kitten, which lived outside, died days later after a struggle with severe intestinal problems. The blobs came again in the rain on August 16, but this time no one in the household fell ill.

There have been no other reports of blob falls in the vicinity, although a National Weather Service employee received a call from an unidentified man in early August describing hot, metallic particles from the sky that burned holes in his children's trampoline.

Dr. David Little, who treated Barclift's mother, said he doubted that Hearn's illness was connected to the blobs—her dizziness and nausea appeared to be caused by an inner ear problem. Nevertheless, he had the stuff analyzed. The lab technician found human white blood cells in it.

Little suggested the blobs might be concentrated fluid waste from an aircraft lavatory, as this would explain the presence of human cells as well as the illnesses. The kitten, he said, could have been hurt by ingesting antifreeze from the waste.

Barclift was unimpressed and called the Federal Aviation Administration in Seattle. Spokesman Dick Meyer ruled out aircraft waste as all commercial plane toilet fluids are dyed blue. "We don't know what it is or where it came from," he said. "It's a puzzle."

The FAA investigator asked the military if there had been any flights over the area or any exercises that might explain the blobs. This is where the jellyfish theory came in, according to Meyer. It's not clear who should get credit for this theory, but it was based on the fact that the blobs appeared around the time that the 354th Fighter Squadron out of McChord Air Force Base was dropping bombs about 10 to 20 miles west of Ocean Shores on the Washington coast. Despite the 40 to 50 miles separating the bombing runs and the blob fallout, the suggestion was made that a school of jellyfish had been blown literally sky-high.

Again, Barclift was unimpressed. Why had the blobs fallen on two occasions, and why only when it was raining? After a week's worth of phone calls to state and federal agencies, she finally persuaded the Washington State Department of Ecology to conduct tests on the blobs.

Mike Osweiler of the Department's hazardous-material unit discovered that the blobs were once alive, or at least part of some living creature. He found a number of cells of different sizes before passing the samples on to the Department of Health, since his unit was not equipped to identify biological cells. The cells had no nuclei, so they weren't human white blood cells. Osweiler had no idea what jellyfish cells looked like.

We have yet to hear if further tests have laid the mystery to rest, but the flying jellyfish theory has certainly found favor with the people of Oakville. Some want to start an annual jellyfish festival where they shoot jellyfish into town with a cannon. The local tavern was also concocting a new drink, "The Jellyfish," made of vodka, gelatin and juice.

METEOROLOGICAL SUPERLATIVES

WEATHERMAN'S WOES

Indian weatherman Cibonco Mala forecast sun and it snowed, while his warning of frost preceded a heat wave. TV chiefs pulled the plug on his New Delhi show when he began crying on screen. He went into hiding after death threats.

CROCS FLOW FREE

A flood in Thailand on September 30 caused 300 crocodiles to escape from flooded reptile farms. Speedboat crews pursued the reptiles with electric prodders, fishing nets and rifles. The hunt spread to Bangkok after unconfirmed sightings of 10-foot crocs in a suburb where dogs have recently disappeared.

There are about a million farmed crocs in the country. The escapes could be a boost for the dwindling number of wild river crocs.

FANS SHOCKED

Lightning struck a crowd of soccer fans in Puerto Lempira, Honduras, on June 3, killing 17 and injuring 35. Eleven died instantly and another six died later at a local clinic. All but one of the victims were Mizkito Indians.

OZONE HOLE

The ozone hole over the Southern Hemisphere has doubled in size in the

HAILSTONE BATTERINGS

❦ Hailstones as big as basketballs as well as a tornado struck the Guangdong province of China (just north of Hong Kong), bringing darkness at noon, 37 dead, 453 injured and 17 missing. Several died from direct hits by hailstones; the heaviest was found in Zhaoqing City and weighed 15 kg (33 pounds). One man was killed by lightning. Others were fatally slammed to the ground by the tornado, which reached a speed of 60 meters per second and pounded some villages for as long as 20 minutes. About 293,000 people were affected, 2,197 houses collapsed, 16,993 houses were damaged and 128 boats capsized. About 34,300 acres were flooded and 35 dams damaged. A week later, six-inch hailstones weighing 680 grams (24 ounces) fell on the city of Fuzhou, injuring 600.

❦ On May 7 a fierce storm, the worst in 20 years, whipped through northern Texas, killing at least 18, injuring more than 100 and leaving three missing. Hailstones, variously described as the size of fists, cricket balls, grapefruit, softballs or baseballs, hit pedestrians, crashed through cars and buildings and lay 2 feet deep in the streets. Grapefruit-sized hailstones put 51 jets and 24 smaller planes out of action at Dallas–Fort Worth International Airport. Hundreds of flights were cancelled.

last year and is now as big as Europe, according to the U.N.'s weather agency.

Levels over Europe and North America have also dropped 10 to 15 percent since depletion began in the 1980s. "Every one percent drop in ozone means roughly 1.3 to 1.5 percent more ultraviolet radiation reaching the surface," said spokesman Rumen Bojkov.

SPONTANEOUS PITS IN OMSK

An unexplained pit discovered in a Russian oat field.

This is one of two enigmatic pits found in October 1994 in a field of oats in the village of Porechiye, which lies in the Muromtsevo district of the Omsk region in Russia. It is 16 feet across and 15 feet deep. The other pit has a smaller diameter, but its depth was unknown, as a weighted 50-foot rope could not reach the bottom. Local residents connect the appearance of the pits with fluorescent objects seen in the sky from time to time.

WEAR LOTS OF LAYERS

Our climate could alter radically in a very short time: ice-core samples from Greenland indicate that the jump from the last Ice Age to the hospitable Holocene took, not centuries, as once believed, but three to seven years.

NOVEMBER BUTTERFLIES IN BRITAIN

1994 was the warmest November in Britain since records began in 1659, shortly after the invention of the thermometer. The mean temperature (10.6°C) was four degrees above normal and more than 1°C warmer than the previous record in 1818. Wildlife was thrown into confusion: butterflies and dragonflies were sighted, roses bloomed and swallows delayed their migration.

SANDSTORM MASSACRES LIVESTOCK

The sandstorm hit the town of Bayanhot in western Inner Mongolia in the afternoon of May 16, and later moved to the northern part of Ningxia. It killed 6,000 livestock and left 105,000 others missing.

MIRACULOUS RAINFALL

Early in August, the district of Barmer in the Thar desert, Northern Rajasthan, India saw rain for the first time since declaring its independence in 1947. People sang and danced and children looked up at the sky in wonder.

LORD SHIVA'S ICICLE WILTS

The Hindu god Shiva appears to have lost his virility this year. An ice phallus or lingam symbolizing his fertility has failed to form in the sacred cave of Amarnath in the Kashmiri Himalayas in India for the first time in living memory. In August, 20,000 devotees joined the annual pilgrimage to the cave, more than 12,000 feet up a mountain, which is accessible for only one month a year. Flanked by soldiers and paramilitary police, they braved hand grenade-lobbing Muslim militants protesting India's rule over Kashmir. Scientists blame the lingam's failure to form on abnormally high temperatures, but pilgrims disagree. "It's a bad omen," said one. "It's Lord Shiva's way of showing his anger about the spread of sin in the world."

TWISTER TOSSES CAR

A twister that flattened parts of the Massachusetts town of Great Barrington on May 29 picked up a car containing two students and a staff member from Eagleton School and hurled it 600 feet into the woods, killing all three. At least 23 others were injured.

STRANGE DEATHS

❂ Inventor Hector Penna spent four years developing a powerful factory cooling fan. He was modifying his invention in his laboratory in San Julian, Argentina, when his wife walked in and flicked on the light switch, not realizing he had connected it to the fan. He was decapitated by the blades.

❂ Florian Iorga, 42, and his son Aurel, 16, were electrocuted by a booby trap they had set up to protect their onion patch in Bucharest, Romania. Hearing noises in the night, they ran out to investigate—and tripped over the cables wired to the mains. The bodies were found by the man's wife. The same fate befell a 49-year-old man in Slatina, Croatia, earlier in the year after he wired up his house and its perimeter against burglars.

❂ Jilted lover Scott McCraw, 37, from Long Island, committed suicide on February 21, 1994, by agitating Shakey, his pet rattlesnake, until it bit him. He died in a field from heart failure while the snake died of hypothermia. The bodies were not discovered for 19 days.

❂ Krzysztof Azninski, 30, had been drinking all day in his garden in Poland with three friends. The four men put on traditional "toughness bonnets" and played macho games. Franciszek Zyzcoszusko, 41, put his hand on a chopping block and dared Azninski to cut it off. Azninski hacked at it with a knife, partially severing the wrist, then put his own head on the block and challenged Zyzcoszusko to chop it off—which he did, with an axe. The revelers then decided things had gone too far, stopped the contest and began to sing a folksong called "Roll the Head of the Giant," which woke the neighbors.

❂ Charles Davies, 67, from Cheltenham in Gloucestershire, England, gave a solo rendition of the old soldiers' song "Goodbye" at the annual dinner of the Cotswold Male Voice Choir in Eckington, Hereford and Worcester, on January 23. He finished with the words: "I wish you all a last goodbye." As the crowd applauded, he collapsed and died.

COSMOLOGICAL SUPERLATIVES

WE'RE LOSING THE MOON

The Earth and Moon have drifted apart by one meter since a mirror was placed on the Sea of Tranquillity by Apollo astronauts Buzz Aldrin and Neil Armstrong in July 1969.

The mirror has been used as a cosmic tape measure by bouncing lasers off it. The Moon is moving four centimeters further away each year due to friction from tides.

Another surprise, said Peter Bender of the University of Colorado, is that the direction of the Moon's axis of rotation changed gradually over a period of 18.6 years, probably as a result of it having a fluid core.

HUBBLE'S HEAVENLY HULA HOOPS

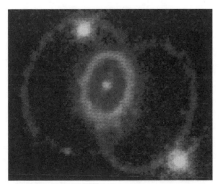

Mysterious space rings many trillion miles wide have mystified astronomers.

The three bright circles pictured above, about three-and-a-half light years across, seen through the Hubble telescope, have been described by an astronomer as "the most stupefying thing I have ever seen." The rings are close to the site of Super-

nova 1987a, which exploded in 1987 about 170,000 light years away in the Greater Magellanic Cloud, the closest supernova to Earth observed since the invention of telescopes.

The explosion had been expected to light up a sphere of gas shed by the star before it blew up. The centers of the two big rings do not align with the site of the supernova. One seems to be a mirror image of the other. The dense inner ring (which had been previously observed) is about one light year in diameter—that's 5.8 trillion miles. Its diameter suggests that it was created about 30,000 years before 1987a blew up.

INTERGALACTIC WATERING HOLE

First came the discovery of a vast cloud of alcohol—an estimated trillion trillion liters of it—surrounding a newly formed star in the constellation of Aquila. Dubbed "the bar at the end of the universe," it was located by British astronomers using the James Maxwell Telescope in Hawaii. In a splendid attempt to make science meaningful to earthbound streetlife, Dr. Geoff MacDonald of the University of Kent said the Scotch mist contains enough alcohol to provide 300,000 pints of beer a day for everyone on this earth for the next billion years.

More merriment was caused by Professor Lewis Snyder of the University of Illinois at Urbana, who revealed that his team had detected a vast cloud of nitrous oxide—the "laughing" gas used by dentists as a general anesthetic—near the center of our own galaxy, the Milky Way. Located in a dust cloud known as Sagittarius B2, several hundred light years in diameter, it also contains cyanide, but not, says Snyder, in concentrations strong enough to amuse or kill.

AMAZING DISCOVERIES

The Aquila constellation was the location of another discovery last year: a blob of matter appeared to be traveling 25 percent faster than the speed of light, one of the supposed universal constants. The group of astronomers who published their findings in *Nature* said they resolved the paradox as an illusion created by the way its speed and direction was perceived from Earth.

Other recent findings include possibly the most massive black hole yet, located in galaxy NGC4258, 21 million light years from Earth, with a mass equal to 40 million Suns; a new spiral galaxy concealed behind the Milky Way (in the Zone of Avoidance, so called because it is so obscured by gas and dust) and named Dwingeloo 1 after the Dutch radio telescope through which it was first seen; and seven new moons of Saturn detected in the 1981 Voyager 2 photos by astronomers at Queen Mary and Westfield College, University of London.

GIANT UFO AHOY!

The tiny announcement in the London Sunday *Times* seemed out of proportion to the import of its content: "An unidentified object that has entered our solar system, mystifying scientists with its huge size, may threaten the end of the planet." Science fiction fans, familiar with the scenario of the aliens arriving in moon-sized ships, may well have wondered if this was the moment when fiction became fact. The feeling was compounded by a large feature, just a few pages away in the same issue, on the story of the Roswell UFO and the putative alien autopsy film. However, while it is true that the newcomer has burst out of the interstellar darkness to catch professional astronomers unawares, puzzling over its unusual size and nature, most astronomers agree it is a very large comet.

It was discovered somewhere between the orbits of Saturn and Jupiter by two amateur astronomers—Alan Hale in New Mexico and Thomas Bopp in Arizona—on July 23. It was their first discovery, although Hale is acknowledged as one of the top comet observers, having studied around 200 known comets.

Within a week, astronomers had made more than 200 observations; enough to determine that Comet Hale-Bopp (or C/1995 01) has a very stretched elliptical orbit of over 3,000 years and will be at its closest to this earth on March 23, 1997, when it will be easily visible in the Northern Hemisphere (although for most of the time it will be best seen from Southern latitudes).

Comet Hale-Bopp is unusually bright for an incoming object so far away, leading early reports to speculate that it might be as much as 1,000 miles across (ie. a hundred times bigger than Halley's comet). The prospect of something so large heading this way triggered the expected Doomsday-style reporting in the populist press. However, there is no chance of it hitting our planet; the official estimate is that the closest it will get to us will be 120 million miles. The actual size of the object is unknown—it could have a small but very active nucleus or a very large nucleus with a small active region—but as it comes closer to our sun it is expected to get brighter and will appear like a star with a tail.

Astronomers have admitted being surprised by the unexpected arrival. "It is unheard of for a comet to be visible by small telescopes while so far away," said

Dr. Brian Marsden of the Harvard-Smithsonian Center for Astrophysics, who suggests it could be "the comet of the millennium," possibly even surpassing the Great Comet of 1811 which turned night into day and which was said to portend the downfall of Napoleon.

PI IN THE SKY

The mysterious mathematical constant "pi" has always been a favorite of cosmologists of every stripe, from probability theorists to explainers of the proportions of the Great Pyramid. Some have found it in the relationship of structures on Mars while others have proposed that the Search for Extraterrestrial Intelligence (SETI) program scan the skies on the wavelength of hydrogen multiplied by pi. "Knowledge of pi would be the signature of a civilization," said Professor David Blair of the University of Western Australia. Now, a research fellow at Aston University, Robert Matthews, has proved that the value of pi can be deduced from studying stars in the night sky. Blair created a list of a million random numbers based on the distances between pairs of stars. Applying "analytical number theory" to pairs of numbers which had no common factors apart from 1, he arrived at a value for pi within five parts per thousand of the standard value. "Truly," says Blair, "pi is in the sky."

DASTARDLY DARK MATTER

"Dark matter" is the stuff we are told makes up over 90 percent of the universe, in order to account for the way galaxies move: there has to be 90 percent more matter than we can see to produce the gravity required to account for movements of visible matter.

Dark matter has always seemed to be the most egregious fudge factor imaginable. It is supposed to make up 90 percent of everything, even though no one has detected it. Furthermore, to make the theories fit, it has to come in hot and cold varieties and form a neat spherical halo round each visible galaxy. Recently, cosmologists have made various attempts to kick dark matter into the cosmic dumper.

First, observations have shown that our galaxy is not only moving with the general expansion of the universe, but is moving at 425 miles per second towards Virgo, a completely different direction. This means there are larger clumps of stuff at greater distances than current theory suggests, making the universe lumpier than thought and undermining the idea of evenly spread dark matter.

Meanwhile, Los Alamos National Laboratory in the U.S. has found that neutrinos, subatomic particles previously thought massless, actually do have a very small mass. These are so common in the universe (there are about a billion in every cubic meter of it) that they can account for all the missing mass of the universe, or 20 percent of it, getting rid of the need for either dark matter entirely, or just the hot dark matter, depending on which report you believe.

SCHWASCAR

THE SCHWASCAR AWARDS

METEORITE CAR CRASH

❂ There are only three recorded reports of meteorites hitting cars. Our favorite instance occurred on June 20, 1994, when José Martin and his wife, Vincenta Cors, were driving from Madrid to Marbella in their BMW. Just south of Getafe, a three-pound meteorite crashed through the windshield on the driver's side. It ricocheted off the dashboard, bent the steering wheel, grazed the little finger of Martin's right hand, bounced off the roof and smashed a camera and loudspeakers in the back window before coming to rest on the back seat. The meteorite was donated to the Museum of Natural Sciences in Madrid, where its extraterrestrial origin was confirmed. It was part of a 130-pound meteorite, and 81 further fragments were found weighing between half an ounce and 11 pounds.

RUNNERS-UP

❂ The first reported incident occurred on October 9, 1992, when a meteorite struck the parked Chevrolet (right) in the New York suburb of Peekskill. The second is our Schwascar winner above.

❂ The third car/meteor collision came this year. High school principal Keiichi Sasatani of Neagari, Japan, noticed a gaping hole in the boot of his car on February 18. He discovered a two-inch-wide meteorite and several smaller fragments embedded in the bottom of the vehicle. Neighbors reported hearing a loud noise late the previous evening.

Michael Aponte shows off the damage to his girlfriend's Chevrolet after it was hit by a meteorite.

OTHER METEORITE NEWS:

❂ During the night of March 4, a farmer in the village of Andechs near Munich in Bavaria reported seeing a 500-foot-high fountain of water and mud. The next day a police helicopter spotted a crater 65 feet wide and 24 feet deep. The police ruled out an aircraft or satellite accident and decided a meteorite had crashed. "Lucky escape for Munich. Meteorite strikes near Lake Ammersee," ran the headline in the local *Abendzeitung*, after which it made the front page of *Bild*, the national tabloid daily. An expert reckoned the meteorite was 200 pounds to 400 pounds in weight—a substantial space boulder. Only it wasn't. The "crater" was the site of an artificial lake for wildlife excavated by the local landowner using 100 kg of explosives. The police had received notice that the blast was to take place on the Monday two days after the event.

GEOPHYSICAL ACTIVITY

LOUD CLEANERS

About half of the 450 top seismologists attending a conference in Wellington, New Zealand, failed to notice a 4.4 Richter earthquake. "Apparently, one or two delegates thought it was just the cleaners," commented one of the organizers.

HEAVY GROCERIES

Providing a puzzle for future archeologists, 300 shopping carts beyond repair were buried in the foundations of a new highway bypass in England.

EARTHQUAKE FLATTENS SETTLEMENT

On May 28, a quake measuring 7.6 on the Richter scale, possibly the worst quake in Russian history, struck the Moscow-controlled island of Sakhalin, north of Japan. The oil-producing settlement of Neftegorsk (pop. 3,500) was flattened and the confirmed death toll by June 9 was 1,841.

GRANDMA MULBERRY PARTS THE WAVES

At sunset on Easter Sunday and Monday (April 16 and 17), an estimated 300,000 people celebrated joyously as the sea parted, revealing a path that only moments before was beneath the waves. "It's like Moses parting the waves," said one woman, only this wasn't the Red Sea long ago but a small strait off the South Korean coast where, every year, a strong tide splits the water between the islands of Jindo and Modo to reveal a 1.7-mile road connecting the two islands. For an hour on two consecutive days every year, thousands of pilgrims attempt to walk the path. Many more are content to enjoy the three-day festival, including the temporary food and medicine stalls along the beach.

Korean tradition attributes the annual "miracle" to Grandma Mulberry, who lived on Jindo 500 years ago in a mountain village that was threatened by tigers. Seeking safety, the villagers one day built a raft, packed up and sailed off to Modo—but in their haste they forgot Grandma Mulberry. She prayed to the Dragon Lord to be reunited with her family. One version of her legend says her wish was granted and she died of happiness, but another has her tarrying too long on the miraculous road, only to be swallowed by the sea.

In a small shrine on the beach is a painting of her dressed in white, her graying hair neatly braided into a bun. Women light incense there as they pray for her intercession. Shamans dance here for good harvests and for success in combating evil forces.

GOLD SPEW

Dr. Fraser Goff, a geologist at the Los Alamos National Laboratory in New Mexico, announced that the Galeras volcano in the Colombian Andes was spewing more than a pound of gold particles into the atmosphere daily in October, and depositing as much as 45 pounds of the metal annually into the rocks surrounding its crater. He estimated that a gold vein at the base of the volcano was at least 10 feet wide. He predicted a gold rush, although mining an active volcano is not recommended.

....

DISASTER POTPOURRI IN PAPUA NEW GUINEA

....

For five days in September the volcanoes Vulcan and Tavurvur spewed smoke, ash and poisonous fumes 55,000 feet into the sky and blanketed the port town of Rabaul, on the island of New Britain, in hot ash, pumice stone and mud up to three feet deep. The previous day, the area was shaken by a quake that was 5.1 on the Richter scale and there were several aftershocks and fierce electrical storms. The port and airport were closed and 30,000 people evacuated. The water in the harbor boiled from volcanic vents, and unexploded Japanese bombs from World War II tunnels were washed down the hills in mudslides. The known death toll was five. Vulcan last erupted in 1937, killing 507 people.

THE
PARANORMAL
WORLD

THE PARANORMAL WORLD

This is the real meat and potatoes of forteana. It covers what Charles Fort liked to call "the damned"—the data that doesn't fit into current scientific theories of the universe. The *X-Files* stuff. There really wasn't a lot of action in the paranormal world last year, though UFO appearances were well up. Good luck was down but, mysteriously, so was bad luck.

PSYCHICAL PHENOMENA

ANCIENT EGYPTIAN IN CUSTODY BATTLE

American "channeler" and former cable TV saleswoman Judith Z. Knight, 46, has won a legal battle for the custody of Ramtha, a 35,000-year-old warrior spirit, after being taken to court by German psychic Julie Ravel, 53, who claimed exclusive rights to the ancient Egyptian (or is he Atlantean?).

Knight told the bemused judge in Linz, Austria: "I've had spiritual contact with Ramtha since 1978. I need him and he needs me." Ravel countered: "Ramtha feeds his thoughts and energies through me and me alone. I am his keeper."

Knight has made a fortune through Ramtha since he supposedly surfaced while she was in her kitchen. Acolytes known as "Ramsters," including until recently the Hollywood actress Shirley MacLaine, flock to her house in Yelm, near Seattle, to see her sink into a hypnotic trance. The gruff voice of Ramtha offers advice on life's timeless mysteries, including how best to invest your money.

Judge Maria Friedinger ruled in Knight's favor, awarding her $900. Ravel, she declared, had infringed copyright by claiming she also had

PECULIAR PRESS

**BLIND RIOTERS
APPREHENDED IN ZAMBIA**
Bangkok Post, March 4, 1994

**MAN CHARGED WITH RAPING DAUGHTER,
MOLESTING SON AND BUGGERING COW**
Cork Examiner, April 26, 1994

**N. KOREAN LEADER NAMES ANCIENT
FROG "ANCIENT FROG"**
Bangkok Post, April 19, 1994

contacted Ramtha while in a Berlin glass shop. Ravel later passed details of this contact to her followers in an Austrian castle, where she runs a parapsychological outfit called Light Oasis.

LAWYERS GAG BARBIE

In the best traditions of Californian infantilism, the giant toy corporation Mattel has thrown a tantrum because a New Age psychic is playing with its dolls. In 1992 "channeler" Barbara Bell of San Francisco began receiving psychic messages from Barbie, the pouting plaything who is 35 years old this year. The first was: "I need respect."

After two years of psychic transmissions, Mattel has put an end to Barbie Channeling Newsletter by threatening a multimillion-dollar lawsuit. Through her psychic guide, Barbie has been answering queries about what life is like when you have a constant smile, a 42-inch bust, a reversible head and legs that are frequently amputated by little brothers. "I go into a light trance and the words come flying out," said Bell, 44. "There are 700 million Barbie dolls in the world with no voice that's real."

On a related matter, senior Kuwaiti religious official, Khaled al-Mathkour, has issued a fatwa calling for the Barbie doll to be banned because, he said, its feminine curves had "nothing to do with childhood."

PIS-SED OFF

According to a program on ARD television in Germany last May, a "Psychotronic Influence System" (PIS) developed by the Soviet KGB in the

1970s that turns people into program-mable "human weapons" is being used today by the Russian police. It relies on hypnosis and high-frequency radio waves and can be activated by code words or ciphers.

PIS was first publicized early this year at a conference in Russia sponsored by Gorbachev's Glasnost Foundation. Those programmed included members of the special forces and regular soldiers in the Afghan conflict, which ended in 1988.

Alexander Kutchurov, the head of Russia's Institute for Parapsychological Research, said that PIS made its subjects incapable of feeling sympathy. Valery Kaniuka, former project leader, now re-grets his role, describing PIS as "the de-struction of the human intellect."

After the existence of the project was made public, hundreds of former Soviet soldiers, police and KGB mem-

WAYWARD TRAVELS

❧ A paternity suit backfired for a hitchhiker in Israel who got pregnant after having sex with the driver who picked her up. She spent three years tracing him and applied for child support; this was the first time the man heard that their brief encounter had made him a father. He and his wife were childless after 20 years of marriage, and he successfully countersued for custody of the child after medical tests confirmed his paternity.

❧ Ian Lewis, 43, of Standish, Lancashire, spent 30 years tracing his family tree back to the 17th century. He traveled all over Britain, talked to 2,000 relatives and planned to write a book about how his great-grandfather left to seek his fortune in Russia and his grandfather was expelled after the Revolution. Then he found out he had been adopted when he was a month old and his real name was David Thornton. He resolved to start his family research all over again.

❧ Sven Harkus, 72, set out from the town of Sundsvall on central Sweden's rolling plains with his 16-year-old grandson on a 60-mile trip to the Jämt-land lakes for a day's fishing. On the way home, they went north instead of south and, despite regularly asking directions, ended up three days later 900 miles away in the Norwegian town of Kirkenes, near the Russian bor-der. The journey came to an abrupt end when Harkus fell asleep at the wheel and crashed into a ditch. Possibly confused by 24-hour summer sun-light, both were convinced that they were near Sundsvall, despite northern Norway's dramatic fjords and mountains. When the police told them where they were, they were treated for shock at the local hospital. A relative was expected in Norway to drive the pair home. Police said they hoped he was a better map reader.

❧ Pop star Lena Fiagbe turned up for the Radio One Roadshow in Bangor. She wandered confused around the North Wales town while the live radio party was in full swing in Bangor, Northern Ireland. What really peeved her was that she had come from Ireland the day before. Thus she lost her chance to sing her smash hit entitled "Got To Get It Right."

bers filed for damages, saying they were psychological wrecks with chronic headaches and hallucinations.

According to Yuri Malin, a former Gorbachev security adviser, the PIS project was begun in response to a similar training scheme launched in America by President Carter. Though Gorbachev halted PIS training in 1988, the technique found its way on to the free market, where mobsters and private security firms are said to be using it. It is also used by special police units before they go into action against drug dealers or demonstrators, according to the tv program, which showed police watching a mesmerizing video in which a seated man apparently utters the activating code words.

....

INGELA'S NIGHT MARE

On the morning of July 10, Ingela Gustavsson, 19, discovered that her horse, a young mare called Unni, was missing from her field in Österbymo in the province of Östergötland, Sweden. A couple of fallen poles in the fence suggested that she had escaped into the forest. Ingela searched all day with the help of neighbors and relatives, but there was no sign of the animal. Advertisements in the local paper and the police failed to help.

"I was out searching every day," said Ingela. "I walked miles and miles in the forest. Then we extended our search by car and drove down small forest roads. The worst of it was the uncertainty, not knowing if anyone had stolen the mare or slaughtered her; or if she had walked into a marsh and drowned."

Weeks passed by with no news. Then, at four in the morning of Saturday, August 19, Ingela started out of her sleep. In a dream she had seen Unni grazing among the megaliths of a monument in the forest called Dackestenar (the Dacke stones) about two kilome-

ters from her home. (Nils Dacke was a 16th-century rebel leader of Småland who fought some battles in Östergötland. We don't know why these prehistoric megaliths have acquired his name.)

Ingela lay awake for two hours thinking about her dream and then called Richard, her boyfriend. He was sleepy and skeptical, but she insisted he come with her to Dackestenar. "We saw at once that the horse had been there," she said. "There were marks in the grass and a couple of yards away, near the river, we found fresh horse droppings."

The horse was found on a path nearby. She was very thin, but unharmed. Six weeks in the forest had made her rather wild, but a bucket of oats Ingela and Richard had brought with them persuaded the animal to return to civilization.

....

THE SEOUL SURVIVORS

....

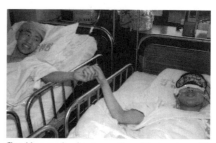

Choi Myong-suk, who ate cardboard for ten days while trapped under concrete in the Sampoong store disaster, holds hands with Yoo Ji-hwan, a fellow survivor.

Sampoong Department Store in Seoul, the capital of South Korea, collapsed on June 29, killing at least 359 people. Conventional wisdom among rescue workers states that after the first 48 hours, there is little chance of finding survivors of this kind of disaster and after a week, serious rescue efforts tend to peter out. But 10 days later, on July 9, Choi Myong-suk, 21, was pulled alive from the rubble after rescue workers heard faint tapping.

LIKE CLOCKWORK

❦ The Commercial Road Baptist Church in Hereford, England, is just below the main police transmission mast, so when the PA system was upgraded, sermons were constantly interrupted. "Echo Alpha, incident at Symonds Rock: climbers in difficulty. Please attend," the PA announced one morning in the middle of Reverend Robert Harris's sermon about Jesus being led up the mountain.

❦ After the world premiere at England's Leeds Playhouse of *The Winter Guest*, a play featuring a community cut off by a blizzard, the audience found themselves snowbound and were put up for the night in the theater.

❦ Dave and Bunny Edgar, married for 67 years, died the same day in different Edinburgh, Scotland, hospitals on March 30, 1994. Bunny, 88, died at 9:30 A.M. and Dave, 90, at 11:57 P.M. without being told of his wife's passing. Jacob and Maria Wiens, both 86 and married for 66 years, died on Christmas Day in St. Catherine's Hospital in Ontario, Canada, Maria 40 minutes after her husband.

❦ World War II veteran Bill Boyes of New Farm, Queensland, couldn't believe his eyes when he looked at the last old-style ticket issued on his bus route before the ticket system was due to be changed. The number was 14496—the same as his old army number.

❦ Abbie Bullivant was born on September 4, 1994, the same date as both her parents, window cleaner Gary, 34, and Jane, 30, of Selly Oak, England. Barbara Gardam of Liverpool gave birth to daughter Cloe on March 2, 1995. Cloe shared her birthday with her elder sisters Stephanie, five, and Kate, two.

❦ Liam Lynch broke his left collarbone after falling from a fence. An hour later, his twin, Aaron, tripped and broke his right collarbone. The six-year-olds, from Cookham Rise, Bucks, also lost the same front teeth in accidents.

❦ Astronomers at Zijinshan observatory at the Chinese Academy of Sciences at Nanjing have discovered a minor planet orbiting the sun which they have called Meizhou, after a town in Guangdong. The small planet, given the international series number 3239, is 328 million kilometers from the sun, which it orbits every 3.23 years.

He had been trapped in a space only four feet wide and had survived by drinking the intermittent trickle of rainwater and eating a cardboard box. Mr. Choi thought that he had been there for only five days. Although he was dehydrated and had lost 11 pounds in weight, otherwise he was in good health.

AGAINST ALL ODDS

❤ Blind Golfer Graham Salmon, 42, scored a hole in one at a 124-yard par three at Fareham, England. The shot secured him fourth place in the British Blind Golf Open.

❤ North Korea's "Dear Leader," Kim Jong Il, is said to have achieved five holes in one in a single round of golf. He also completed the 18-hole Pyongyang course in 34 strokes—25 shots better than the previous world record. This incredible feat was reported by the club's professional, Park Young Nam.

❤ The odds were with Barbara Newell in an Adelaide, Australia casino when she threw 21 consecutive tails in a two-up ring— a four million-to-one occurrence. Sadly, she won only $262.50 instead of a fortune because she did not change her original bet.

The day before the rescue, an expert in *ki* (life force radiance), Lim Kyong-taek, professor of political science at Mokpo University, had told rescuers that a young man was alive in the rubble. Standing silently on the site, he pinpointed the most unlikely place for a survivor—the center of the rubble— and said a piece of heavy machinery should be moved. At first no one was found and the professor left, muttering: "It is strange." But 12 hours later, Mr. Choi was found at the spot indicated.

Two days later, Yoo Ji Hwan, 18, was unearthed not far from where Mr. Choi had been found. She had survived by sipping rainwater from a blanket. Miss Yoo, too, was in good health, despite an acute kidney problem caused by dehydration and malnutrition.

Another four days passed and then rescue workers found Park Seung-hyung, 19, who had been trapped face-down for 16 days under concrete slabs. She was naked, having peeled off her clothes to survive the heat, and had had no food or water. "A monk appeared in dreams from time to time," she told her father. "He gave me an apple and this kept my hope alive." She was rescued underneath a collapsed elevator shaft, not far from the other two survivors. Like Miss Yoo, she had a kidney problem but otherwise she was "in fairly good condition."

A young road worker survived 40 days' entombment in 1994 after a landslide near the Wu River in China's Sichuan province on April 30. Zeng Shuhua, 20, weighed only 30 kilos by the time peasants heard his groans and called for help. He had had no food and only a trickle of water.

PROPHECIES

STAR-CROSSED CROSSWORD

The solution to the British *Daily Telegraph's* crossword No. 21,362 on September 24, 1994, included the words "passenger list," "slain," "master mariner" and "Estonia." Four days later, at 12:30 A.M. on September 28, the ferry *Estonia* sank in the Baltic with nearly 1,000 passengers on board. There were about 140 survivors. It was Europe's worst transport disaster since 1945.

The case has distinct echoes of the *Telegraph's* Overlord crosswords, which included several of the code words for the D-Day landings in 1944.

DEATHS FORESEEN

Twelve-year-old Richard Meese from Wordsley, England, liked to make tape recordings in his bedroom, pretending he was a radio DJ. In the fall of 1992 he was knocked down when a young woman sped through a red traffic light in her Metro and struck him. He was rushed to the hospital, where he died of head injuries. About three days after his death, his mother, Linda, went upstairs and put on one of his tapes, just to listen to his voice.

The tape she played, made six weeks before the accident, contained a chillingly accurate premonition. In a 10-minute interlude between music and jokes, the boy describes, in a somber but firm voice, a car coming towards him driven by a woman. It hits him. He is taken to a large building like a warehouse and he can't open his eyes properly. He says that one arm hurts, but that his legs are not injured—an accurate description of his injuries. The account ends: "They put me in a wooden box. They stripped me naked...Goodbye." His mother said that when she saw him in the hospital, he was unclothed. "The whole thing is uncanny," she said, "because Richard never spoke about death."

This sad tale is reminiscent of another premonition. On September 21, 1992, carpenter David Swankie, 36, from Birmingham, England, was killed on the A38 near Lichfield.

Swankie was hurled through the windscreen of a Leyland truck in torrential rain when it plowed into a Nissan pickup which had broken down at Barton-under-Needwood.

The previous night, according to his common-law wife Margot Ahern, he had a dream about a highway accident in which he killed a child. He decided not to drive, so his friend Chris Wood was at the wheel; but he was unable to avoid his appointment with the Grim Reaper. No child was injured in the accident, so the premonition was slightly off beam.

FATAL STARS

Researchers at the University of California, San Diego, appear to have discovered a curious correlation between belief in Chinese astrology and survival times in major illnesses. According to traditional Chinese belief, persons born in a year corresponding calendrically to the element fire fare worse than others with heart conditions; Earth year individuals are more prone to cancers; metal year people do worse with bronchitis and asthma, and so on.

David P. Phillips and coworkers studied death records of 28,169 adult

Californian Chinese and 412,632 Caucasian controls of individuals dying between 1969 and 1990. The degree to which the Chinese believed in astrology was assumed from whether or not they had autopsies performed; autopsies being shunned by believers in traditional Chinese medicine. Women were also assumed to have a stronger belief in Chinese tradition than men.

The results showed that Chinese people born in Earth years suffering from lung cancer died 1.6 years earlier than Chinese people born in other years. Chinese Earth year women died 3.3 years earlier than other Chinese cancer victims, and metal year women suffering from bronchitis, emphysema or asthma died 8.3 years earlier than all other Chinese people with similar illnesses. Overall, Chinese people with astrologically correlated illnesses died from 1.3 to 4.9 years sooner than other Chinese people born outside ill-fated years. Similar correlations do not appear among the Caucasian controls.

The researchers conclude that psychosomatic factors can markedly affect the longevity of patients; if you believe in the astrological inevitability of the illness being fatal, you die quicker. What they haven't concluded is that Chinese astrology might actually work, and that you may actually die quicker anyway. Guess it just depends on what you want to believe!

SAY WHAT?

❦ Multiple sclerosis sufferer Mary Clamser, 42, was wheelchair-bound for 23 years and lost all sensation in her legs two years ago. At the end of last year, she was struck by lightning and knocked out as she grasped a shower door at her home in Oklahoma City. When she came to in hospital, sensation had returned to her legs. Within weeks, she was back on her feet.

❦ Lucy Benawell, 28, a secretary from Philadelphia, makes glass break when she stands near it for more than a minute. Unnamed doctors blame "an unusual electric charge in her body."

❦ Tucked away in a football report in England's *Whitby Gazette* on March 24, 1994, was the following: "Whitby keeper Paul Robinson was taken to hospital at half-time and detained overnight when he suffered memory loss. 'He couldn't remember anything about the game, it was really strange,' said secretary Charlie Woodward. 'But there was no sign of injury apart from two small marks on his neck.' "

APPARITIONS

TRICKY DICK RIDES AGAIN

Ever since President Nixon was entombed at the Richard Nixon Library and Birthplace in California on April 26, 1994, odd nocturnal manifestations have been reported.

A night watchman has claimed to have seen a luminous green mist over the president's grave. Once he saw a man enter the Nixon birthplace house, but when he went to arrest the culprit no one was found there and the door was locked. He has also heard tapping sounds emanating from the Watergate display room. On several occasions, the audiotape machines that play the Watergate tapes have malfunctioned.

Is the restless spirit of the old crook trapped on the Earthly plane? Listen closely at the fence in the dead of night.

GHOST PLANE MYSTIFIES POSTMAN

In May 1994 postman Tony Ingle, 51, and his wife, Susan, were staying in their camper at Laneside, England, on the Derbyshire moors. On the sunny afternoon of Friday, May 5, Mr. Ingle was out walking along nearby Aston Lane with his eight-year-old retriever, Ben. Sometime between 4:40 and 5 P.M. he saw a huge Second World War airplane, only 40 to 60 feet above the moors and banking to the left, clearly in trouble.

"I was so convinced it was going to crash," he said. "I raced 100 yards up the lane to a gateway and the plane went out of sight. I expected to see the wreckage, but there was nothing, just an eerie silence and the sheep grazing. Then I realized as I calmed down a bit

that although I had seen the propellers turning, the plane had been absolutely silent." Tony saw the plane in such detail that he was later able to identify it from pictures as a Dakota.

Research at the *Sheffield Journal* showed that Mr. Ingle's sighting was just 50 yards from where a USAF Dakota crashed in heavy mist in July 1945. All seven crew died. In the last week of June, a plaque commemorating the dead airmen and the six-man crew of a Royal Canadian Air Force Lancaster which crashed near the same spot a few weeks earlier, on May 18, 1945, killing all six crew, was unveiled 1,800 feet up on Bleaklow moor.

Mr. Ingle's sighting was not the first. Over the last 30 years, several people claim to have seen ghostly aircraft in the area.

"I don't believe in ghosts," said Mr. Ingle. "I am just not that type. I can't explain what I saw and I find it very disturbing. Since it happened, the dog will not go up the lane." He told *FT* that he only rang up the *Sheffield Journal* to help him explain the incident, and didn't wish the details to appear in the paper. The story subsequently appeared in the *Daily Sport* and a Northern Irish paper, and his phone had been red hot. His colleagues at work had ribbed him and he was heartily sick of the whole affair.

ONE DOG NIGHT

Glasgow architect David Roulston spent the night in the reputedly haunted Mary King's Close in Edinburgh, Scotland, and managed to raise $7,500 for the BBC's Children-in-Need appeal.

"I had a camcorder with me in the Close and at one point I felt quite

VAMPIRE-IN-TRAINING

❦ Sally Fahy, 22, went to a Toronto bar with musician Donald Kuntz on October 23, 1992. When Kuntz said, "I'll get you drunk if you let me suck your blood," Fahy thought he was joking, but when they went back to her apartment she nonetheless looked for a penknife to cut herself. Kuntz then produced a butcher's knife from his track pants, made a deep cut in her right wrist and began sucking. Fearing that she would die, she broke free and admitted herself to the hospital. In March 1993, Kuntz was sentenced to just one day in jail. The judge said that Fahy had agreed to get drunk, get cut and let him drink her blood. The pair exchanged love letters while he was in jail and they were considering marriage.

RUNNERS-UP

❦ A vampire was exposed in the town of Vannarapettai in Tamil Nadu state, southern India, when a woman complained to police that her husband had been regularly removing blood from her arm with a syringe and drinking it mixed with alcohol.

❦ Police in Vladivostok, Russia, arrested a "vampire woman" who was accused of stabbing a traffic policeman to death in her home and drinking the blood pouring from his wounds while stunned party-goers looked on. The witnesses described the woman as "highly excited."

❦ The aptly-named Benjamin Peck, 18, was jailed for 10 years by Luton Crown Court in England for slashing a 15-year-old boy's neck with a razor and sucking his blood while he was high on drugs. Peck, who left his victim for dead, believed that sucking human blood would give him the strength to sort out his problems. He told psychiatrists that his girlfriend was a vampire and that the Yardies were out to get him.

❦ Ivo Simanis, 34, was arrested in Riga, the Latvian capital, after a young girl was found unconscious and bleeding. Simanis had lured her to his house, where he cut her with razor blades and whipped her with a belt. She escaped by pretending to be dead. Simanis admitted he often drugged children to drain their blood and drink it. He said he got into the habit at the age of 14 and asked to be sentenced to death.

❦ Akhmat Azimov, 24, was sentenced to death in Andizhan, Uzbekistan, for raping, killing and drinking the blood of four boys. He told the court: "I abducted handsome little kids—only boys."

cold," said Mr. Roulston, 47. "I didn't realize what I'd shot until I played it at home and it looked as if there was a head on the wall. To me it looks like the head of a dog—a ghostly apparition. It just seemed to turn and disappear."

Mary King's Close was abandoned following the plague of 1645. The Royal Exchange, which later became the City Chambers, was built over it 120 years later. *Satan's Invisible World Discovered,* a book published in 1685, records a demonic parade of apparitions which forced locals to flee the Close in terror some years previously. An elderly lawyer, Thomas Coltheart, and his wife refused to leave and were almost driven mad by terrifying images of floating limbs, the bodiless phantom of a child, and the "grotesque and monstrous form" of a dog which curled itself up on a chair.

Mr. Roulston's video was edited by student Richard Adamson, 22, who said: "Strange sounds kept appearing and I am convinced the speech and music changed tracks...it only happened round the bit with the ghost."

GHOST SUSPECT IN BISTRO BLAZE

Firemen were puzzled by a blaze in April 1994 at the Same Yet Inn, Simister Lane, in Prestwich, near Manchester, England. Most of the bistro was destroyed at the 268-year-old pub, but one wall was completely untouched. Kevin and Jacqueline Fallon, tenants at the pub for the last 10 years, thought it must have been "the ghost."

"We came down in the morning to

find the wreckage," said Mrs. Fallon. "The room seemed to have smoldered away; but it was stone-cold to the touch. One wall was unaffected. That was the spot where we found the outline of a man when we stripped off the old wallpaper. We have known for some time that the pub was haunted. I saw the ghost myself at 4:30 one morning. At first I felt a presence and then I saw a man, who appeared to be about 60, with a beard and ruddy complexion.

"A couple of years ago a fortune teller came to the pub. After she left, the table and chair where she had been sitting burned to cinders; but the knife and fork and pepper pot on top were unmarked. We have had people staying who have told of strange noises and things moving. The ghost has become quite well-known all over town. The cash till sometimes opens on its own, the music goes up in volume for no reason, and people have seen bottles fall off the shelves and land standing up."

According to local legend, the ghost is James Heyward, a farmer who was attacked by robbers on his way back from the cattle market in 1843. A thorn pierced his throat and he bled to death.

IMAGES

NICE TO SEE ME

Adrian Brown—original or doppelgänger?

A dramatic doppelgänger tale appeared in the *Poole and Dorset Advertiser* on November 3, 1994. Columnist David Haith pointed out that the witness, Adrian Brown, from Heathwood Road, Winton, England, was not a publicity-seeker: "If I hadn't heard a rumor and sought him out this story would remain untold." Four years ago, Mr. Brown worked for a security firm. His job entailed driving around to check on various sites. He ran on a strict timetable, but one night, on his way to a gravel pit, he was delayed by 20 minutes.

At a traffic circle near Holton Heath (not far from Wareham), lit up in the headlights of a truck, he saw a white van identical to the one he was driving, with the same black lettering on the side. The driver turned his head towards him and he saw that it was himself. "I cannot describe the uneasy feeling in that split second we looked at each other," said Mr. Brown. "It was an emotion which started in the pit of my stomach that I have never experienced before."

He drove on, checked the site and went home, feeling stunned and frightened. He knew the firm had another van, but it was broken down and off the road. It occurred to him that his double was at the exact spot he would have been—and had been every night for five months—if he hadn't been late. "What if I'm not really here and the guy driving the other van is the real Adrian?" pondered the perplexed man.

A report in the *British Journal of Psychiatry* in November 1994 examined 56 doppelgänger episodes. A former pilot saw himself several yards away for about 10 minutes. A retired doctor saw an image of himself walk across a room and another man hurried out of a café after seeing a phantom figure looking in from the street.

FANCY MEETING YOU HERE

Cookie Richardson meets her newfound brother, James Austin.

James Austin and Yvette (Cookie) Richardson worked side by side for two years at Philadelphia's main post office before discovering that they were brother and sister. Their parents had separated 33 years earlier, when James was seven months old. He was raised by his paternal grandparents in North Philadelphia while Yvette stayed with her mother in South Philadelphia. They went to school within blocks of each other, both studied accounting and both ended up on the 4 P.M. shift at the post office, which has 4,100 employees.

Their reunion was brought about last June by shop steward Barrie Bowens. Austin had told her that his father died young and that he never knew his mother. Bowens asked for his mother's name and he said Veronica Potter— which Bowens knew was the name of Richardson's mother. She broke the news to Richardson, who then noticed the stunning resemblance between her coworker and an old picture of her father.

CLOSE FAMILY

Tony Munden, 26, of Clevedon Road, Weston-super-Mare, England, discovered he had two half-sisters after receiving a letter from his long-lost mother last Christmas. A trail of enquiry ended at the house next door, where his half-sister Lorraine, 23, was living. Their bedroom windows face each other 15 feet apart, and a waist-high stone wall is all that separates the front gardens. The pair had been neighbors for three months without knowing of each other's existence.

Their mother, Brenda, 47, split up with Tony's father when Tony was 18 months old. She emigrated to South Africa with her daughters Lorraine and Paula from a second failed marriage and now lives near Johannesburg with her third husband, Derek, 35, and younger daughter, Paula, 21.

Tony, a self-employed laborer, said: "I've had to look after myself ever since my father left me when I was 10 and I was taken into care. Now at last I have something to look forward to and family to care about."

PARALLEL MICHELLES

Mother of two Michelle Samways was caught up in a spot of trouble— with mother of two Michelle Samways. The two women moved into numbers 5 and 6 Longstone Close, Portland, England, in October 1994 and hardly a day goes by without a mix-up of some kind. They discovered that they share the same name only when they entered a raffle at a toddlers' group. The two Michelles, aged 26 and 27, were both named after the 1965 Beatles song. They are the same height and build, with similar color and length of hair.

VIRGIN BLOOD FLOODS ITALY

A 17-inch plaster statue of the Blessed Virgin Mary was bought at the Marian shrine of Medjugorje in Herzegovina in 1994 by an Italian priest called Father Pablo Martin, who gave it to his friend and neighbor, electrician Fabio Gregori, 32. The statue was then installed in a specially-built niche in Gregori's garden in the port of Civitavecchia, population 52,000, 50 miles north of Rome.

On February 2, Gregori announced that the statue had started to weep dark red tears. His five-year-old daughter, Jessica, was the first to notice the phenomenon. Thousands of pilgrims flocked to watch; witnesses claim to have seen the liquid flow from the eyes of the statue for about five minutes, nine times in one day. Four days later, the local bishop, Girolamo Grillo, confiscated and hid the statue just before national TV could get a good look. Coachloads of tourists continued to pour into Civitavecchia to worship at the grotto where the statue had once stood. By Good Friday, April 14, the statue was said to have wept 14 times.

In the subsequent two months, there were 10, 13 or 15 similar cases across Italy (reports vary); the phenomenon resembled the moving statue mania that swept across Ireland in 1985. Some commentators put it down to worry about Italy's economic and political turmoil.

The Madonna of Sant'Agostino at Civitavecchia has been weeping bloody tears since February.

In Subiaco, east of Rome, a statue emitted a substance for 10 days that was later identified by biologists as human pus. There were religious exudations at Bergamo and Laziso in the north of Italy and in Castovillari in the deep south. On March 6, a plaque of the famous stigmatic Padre Pio in southern Salerno began to secrete a blood-like substance at the ribs—hundreds went to view.

On March 22, a bas-relief of the Virgin in the entrance hall of a block of flats in Tivoli, just east of Rome, began weeping, prompting a steady stream of visitors—even after the plaque was removed for tests three days later. Meanwhile in Taranta Peligna, in the Abruzzi mountains, a statue bought in Lourdes developed bloodstains on its face,

throat, breasts and hands. In Naples, hundreds of people prayed outside the house of a bedridden man who claimed to have a lacrimatory Madonna in his house. He declined to hand it over to a local priest.

At the end of February, a laboratory report concluded that the liquid coming from the Virgin of Civitavecchia was human blood, group A—but curiously, it was male. Scientists had allegedly X-rayed the statue seven times and found no trace of trick devices. Bishop Grillo, initially skeptical, announced on TV that the statue wept blood on March 15 while he held it, an event witnessed by his sister, brother-in-law and two Romanian nuns. "My sister touched it," he said. "She was braver than me and she ended up with blood on her finger...I saw a tear drop from the eyes of the statue and trickle slowly down to its neck." The bishop's sister said the drop on her finger mysteriously vanished before her eyes. Local people began building parking lots, lavatories and facilities for the disabled in anticipation of a flood of Easter pilgrims.

Grillo planned to unveil the Madonna in time for a special Good Friday parade and 50 unemployed people were hired to spruce up the tiny church of Sant'Agostino where the statue was to be enshrined behind bullet-proof glass. However, the town's chief prosecutor, Antonio Albano, insisted the statue be kept hidden until further checks for fraud were carried out: comparing the DNA of the bloody tears with that of the Gregori family, for instance. Abuse of "public credulity" is a crime in Italy. On April 11, Grillo quoted the Pope as comparing Albano to Communist authorities in the pontiff's Polish homeland, who in 1967 seized a copy of the icon of the black Madonna of Czestochowa, Poland's most sacred shrine. The statue was released on April 18, possibly after overtures from the Vatican. We await developments.

MEDICAL MISHAP

☻ Merryl Baker found three teeth in a chocolate bar called Galaxy Double Nut & Raisin. She complained to Mars, the manufacturers, and the story was reported in the *Daily Star*. Ms. Baker then visited the dentist, where she was told that three of her back teeth were missing. "It was my mistake and I feel such a fool," she said.

RUNNER-UP

☻ Just before he went into surgery on February 20 Willie King joked with the staff at University Community Hospital in Tampa, Florida, to be sure they knew which foot they were going to amputate. Surgeon Rolando Sanchez got it wrong. King, a 51-year-old diabetic, awoke to find he still had his gangrenous right foot. He eventually had both legs cut off just below the knee and settled with the surgeon for $250,000. After the accident, the hospital started a new policy of writing the word "No" on patients' limbs that are not to be amputated.

OTHER INJURIES

☻ Edward and Elizabeth Brimble took their Labrador-mix dog, Trudie, for her daily exercise in Bungay, England, last January. When Trudie began to snarl and foam at the mouth, the Brimbles thought she was having a fit and pinned her down on the road for 10 minutes as she howled and suffered convulsions. It was only after she had died and Mr. Brimble gave her a farewell stroke that he received an electric shock and realized that the ground was "live." Corroded wiring in a lamppost was sending up to 240 volts through the concrete. The Brimbles escaped electrocution because they were wearing rubber boots.

☻ Army bomb disposal experts were called in when a suspicious box was noticed outside Bristol Zoo in England. After it was blown up, it was found to contain a rat left by its owner who was looking for a new home for his pet.

TEARS FOR VEGAS

In September, a statue of the Virgin of Guadalupe could be observed weeping in the backyard shrine of Pablo Covarrubias, behind a branch of 7-Eleven near the intersection of Las Vegas and Lake Mead Boulevards in Las Vegas. The tears started on May 30, 1993. Covarrubias's niece, Martha Saldivar, first saw the statue cry, but few believed her until Channel 8 TV news turned up and documented the event on video. The statue seems to weep only in the presence of Martha. When *FT's* Vegas correspondent Jeffrey Vallance asked why the Madonna cries, she declared: "Our Lady cries to bring the people of Las Vegas back to their faith!" The whole household has become devout.

Other witnessed wonders include the scent of roses and the statue turning and moving forward. A little angel under the statue has been seen getting a "greasy head." On June 17, 1993, a very windy day in Las Vegas, a Marian apparition slowly floated down from heaven in the form of a fine mist. Various miraculous healings are claimed, such as the disappearance of water on the brain and cancerous lesions. Vallance himself witnessed some tears of the Virgin, which were presented to him on a cotton ball.

JESUS FIGURE JOLTS JUDGE

This image in a marble pillar was a spiritual beacon for Cincinnati judge Leslie Gaines.

Judge Leslie Isaiah Gaines was 50 pounds overweight and worried about his high blood pressure. In September 1993, as he struggled up the steps in Hamilton County Courthouse, Cincinnati, he saw the face above on a marble pillar. "I saw the crown of thorns, a bloodstained eye, his beard, the look of sorrow on his face," said the judge. "I felt I got a wake-up call from God."

He told no one except his wife until the following March when he faxed reporters announcing that the image had given him inspiration every day. Before the announcement, some had suggested the face resembled Captain John J. Desmond, an Ohio National Guard officer killed on March 28, 1884, defending the courthouse from a lynch mob. Desmond's statue is in the building's lobby and the judge sent out his fax on the 110th anniversary of Desmond's death.

RIVERS OF BLOOD

From 1981 to 1989, seven young "visionaries" in the Rwandan village of Kibeho claimed to have had visions in which the Blessed Virgin and Christ appeared to them with messages. In one of these visions, which reportedly lasted eight hours, the visionaries were terrified by scenes of a river of blood, abandoned corpses and people killing one another. Inevitably, the interest in these visions grew considerably in the wake of 1994's genocide and refugee migration.

There are close parallels with the Marian apparitions in Medjugorje, Croatia. The Medjugorje visions started on June 24, 1981, those in Kibeho on November 28 that same year. Messages from the Blessed Virgin in both places were broadly similar. In both countries, the apparitions involved young witnesses and were followed by "ethnic cleansing." In both, there were hints of the coming violence, but the larger purpose of such apparitions is generally considered to be a worldwide call to repentance and conversion. The Church has given approval for the faithful to make pilgrimages to Kibeho to venerate the Blessed Virgin. An account of the visions by the Reverend Gabriel Maindron has been published in French.

BAD LUCK

HIGHWAY TO HELL

Residents along Route 666 believe the fact that the road bears the Number of the Beast of Revelation explains its plague of death and destruction. The road runs 200 miles from Monticello in Utah's Mormon country, through the sagelands of southern Colorado and on to Gallup, New Mexico. There are a large number of drunk-driver and hit-and-run killings and the road even has its own serial killer—the Mad Trucker, who police suspect runs people over for sport. In Oliver Stone's bloodfest *Natural*

A SEA OF COINCIDENCE

❤ Strange coincidences, such as meeting someone with the same name or birthday, are more common than most of us think, according to a study by Robert Matthews, a visiting research fellow at Aston University, Birmingham, England, and psychologist Dr. Susan Blackmore. The study, published recently in the journal *Perceptual and Motor Skills,* says that few people have any clear grasp of probability, making them prone to give a paranormal explanation to an apparently strange event. The researchers asked 120 people to answer a simple question: How many randomly chosen people must be brought together for at least an even chance that two of them will share a common trait, such as a star sign, a birthday, or having gone to the same secondary school?

There are 12 star signs, 365 days in the year, and 5,000 secondary schools in England. Five people are needed to give 50:50 odds of sharing a star sign, just 23 are needed to give the same odds of sharing a birthday, and only 85 to give the same odds of having been to the same secondary school.

Many people, presented with the question about schools, simply divide the number of schools by two and suggest that 2,500 people would have to be present; but this is 30 times greater than the necessary minimum. The reason is that these coincidences don't need a match with a specific school.

All that is being asked is that among all the possible pairings that can be made among all the people present, two will be the same.

"It's not surprising we're poor at assessing coincidences," said Dr Blackmore. "Humans typically acquire skill at something by constant practice, but we don't go around all day deliberately seeking out coincidences. If we did, we'd soon realize we live in a sea of them and would be far less surprised when they popped up."

Born Killers, psychopaths Mickey and Mallory kill 52 people along Route 666.

It was road engineers in the 1930s who called the highway Route 666 as the sixth to cross fabled Route 66 between Chicago and Los Angeles. Now a coalition of Bible-belters and Navajo Indians—whose reservation is split by the road—want the name changed. The number is double trouble for the Navajos: not only are many of them literalist Christians, but in traditional belief the number six is considered evil. Navajo spokesman William Lee blamed the road for the popularity of devil worship among local teens and the ritual sacrifice of dogs and cats.

Skeptics blame the accidents on poor lighting, narrow bends and the fact that the road links the reservation, where alcohol is banned, with the nearest bars in Gallup.

GIFT-BEARING TWINS TWINE AUTOMOBILES

Lavinia and Lorraine Christmas spent Christmas Day in Queen Elizabeth Hospital in Kings Lynn, England, being treated for chest injuries, whiplash and concussion. On the morning of Christmas Eve, 1994, the 31-year-old identical twins, who live in different Norfolk villages, decided simultaneously to visit each other to deliver Christmas presents. Their cars ran into each other on a narrow, icy lane at Flitcham. Both cars were write-offs. As the twins' father was already in the same hospital after a knee operation, their mother decided she might as well have her Christmas lunch in the ward with the rest of the Christmases.

PINCHED PARTS

❦ Pensioner Ron Tupper got his balls trapped between the slats of a patio chair after taking a shower at his home in Eastbourne, England. The fire brigade tried grease and other lubricants, and finally freed him after an hour by using cutting equipment to demolish the chair.

❦ Cricketer Mark Hubbard, 29, from Seaton in Devon, England, who weighs 238 pounds, slipped from a sightscreen he was repairing and was left hanging painfully by his scrotum from a hook. He hauled himself off and was driven to a health center where he had seven stitches. "He's sore," said his wife Karen, "but everything's in working order."

❦ Robert Cheuvront, 33, took an early-morning dip in a motel pool in Lakeland, Florida, and was trapped in the shallow end for three hours after getting his penis stuck in the suction filter. At 4:45 A.M. the night clerk heard his cries and help was summoned. The swollen penis was finally extricated from the filter by an ambulance crew using lubricant.

GOOD LUCK

THE GREAT WHITE HOPE

"Miracle" is thought by some Native Americans to be the second coming of White Buffalo Calf Woman.

Native Americans have hailed the birth of a white buffalo (more properly North American bison) as a major religious event, the long-prophesied return of White Buffalo Calf Woman.

"This is like the second coming of Christ on the island of America," said Sioux medicine man Floyd Hand. "The legend is that she would return and unify the nations of the four colors—black, red, yellow and white."

The white cow calf, named Miracle, was born on August 20, 1993, at David Heider's farm near Janesville, Wisconsin. Heider, who keeps 14 buffalo along with conventional cattle, was telephoned by spiritual leader Looks For Buffalo from Pine Ridge South Dakota. The elder had received "signs" that Buffalo Woman would soon return. He said Miracle was born on a white man's farm as "an omen to the white people" and prophesied that her father would die, so that she might live. Two days later, Marvin, the bull that sired her, died of stomach ulcers.

Tribal representatives from all over America have visited the farm and performed religious ceremonies. The last white bison was Big Medicine (1933–1959), but he was disqualified because he was a male. White bison were rare even when 60 million of them roamed the Great Plains. Today, there are only about 130,000 head on American farms, up from 500 at the turn of the century.

Miracle is not an albino; she has brown eyes and a brown muzzle. She may take on a browner shade when she sheds her coat next spring, although she appears to be too white for this to happen. Genetic tests will confirm whether she has any trace of domestic cattle in her ancestry.

TAKE FIVE

Alasdair Lennox of Cromer, England, and his wife, Vivienne, both 31-year-old doctors, had identical twin daughters Katie and Emma in 1991. Now Vivienne has given birth to triplet daughters, all without fertility treatment. At least two, Laura and Claire, are identical. Tests are underway to discover if the third, Hannah, is also identical. The odds of having girl twins followed by girl triplets is around 20 million to one. We are told that identical twins and triplets in succession is unprecedented in medical literature.

SAVED BY THE BELL

Two-year-old Kolby Grinston set off a fire alarm at Kiddie Kove Nursery in Chicago and marched out with his classmates as they had been trained to do. Moments later, a car ran through a red light and struck a second car, which smashed into the nursery as the children

ALL IN THE TIMING

❂ A ceremony to mark the 200th anniversary of a wooden bridge in Montreux, Switzerland, ended abruptly when it collapsed, throwing onlookers into the river.

❂ In Las Vegas, Nevada, four illegal aliens were deported to Mexico in July 1994 after being turned in by the customer for whom they were installing a carpet. Their customer was a certain Arthur Strapp, head of the local office of the U.S. Immigration and Naturalization Service (INS). Commented Strapp: "Out of 900,000 people in Las Vegas, they picked my house."

❂ Sandra Robertson, 32, waited all day for the green carpet she'd chosen to be fitted at her home in Buckinghamshire, England. Eventually she called Allied Carpets, who called the freelance fitter on his mobile phone just as he was putting the finishing touches on the carpet in a bungalow with the same number in nearby Hardwick Road. He had been let into the empty property by an electrician who was working there. By coincidence, the front room had been cleared of furniture and so the fitter set to work.

❂ Mrs. Moira Poor, 69, entered the elevator at the Auckland City Council parking lot in New Zealand on Friday afternoon, December 9, 1994, and was trapped after it stuck between floors. The emergency alarm didn't work because the batteries were dead and there was no telephone. Mrs Poor was carrying nothing but her handbag. She slept on the floor and spent the weekend standing, often yelling for help. On Monday morning, after 67 hours, maintenance workers repaired the elevator. Mrs. Poor went to the car and drove out, but its parking ticket had expired. The booth operator refused to believe she had been trapped for three days and made her pay an excess charge. "I tried to explain," she said. "But the attendant said I stank and ought to be ashamed of myself." A few days later, the city council awarded her $2,100 and free parking in Auckland for life.

❂ Honduran peasant Gustavo Adolfo Amador, now 57, was charged in 1975 with stealing colored pencils from a marketplace in the capital of Tegucigalpa, but a court acquitted him the following year. The written release order, however, didn't arrive at Tegucigalpa's central penitentiary. Amador was released in April 1994, after 19 years inside.

stood outside. The car plowed through a play area and came to a halt on top of several lockers used by the youngsters.

The school's director said the children would have been at the lockers putting away their jackets if Kolby hadn't pulled the alarm.

The story doesn't end there. A van hit by the second car bumped into the youngsters going back into the school. Fourteen children aged four to six were slightly injured; one suffered a broken leg.

JET BOAT FLOAT

An aluminum jet boat, *The Classic*, slipped its moorings on the coast of Western Australia in August 1994 and was found seven months later washed up on a beach in Mozambique, some 5,000 miles away across the Indian Ocean.

On March 31, two fishermen asked Kathleen Brennan, an Australian backpacker visiting Mozambique, if she could identify the papers found in the boat. In an astonishing coincidence, she recognized them as belonging to her neighbor, Denis Bennetts.

Bennetts, a retired crayfisherman of Ledge Point, north of Perth, was told that the $34,000 boat had been seen drifting about 300 miles offshore three weeks after it disappeared. "I thought that was the end of it," he said. One report estimated that the 33-foot boat made the journey by drifting at one mph on the South Equatorial Current.

MUSICAL SHOPPING BAGS

Katie Pierce, of Yarralumla, Australia, put her shopping down at a washbasin in the busy public lavatories in Canberra on December 6, 1994. When she got home, she realized she had picked up someone else's carrier bag by mistake. Hers was a Grace Brothers' bag and now she had a DJs one. It didn't really matter, because the stranger had bought exactly the same items she had: one Gary Larson desk calendar, one Anne Geddes baby calendar and one pair of boxer shorts; her shorts had had the Phantom on them, these had Yogi Bear.

MIRACLES

STRIKING LUCKY

Veronica Ron, a 16-year-old Swedish student, was blown out of these boots by a lightening bolt.

At the end of July, 1994, Veronica Ronn, 16, was keeping goal at a soccer game in Gavie, 90 miles north of Stockholm, Sweden, when a violent thunderstorm rolled across the pitch. Veronica was struck by lightning, blown out of her boots and hurled into the air. Her heart stopped for four minutes, but a teacher administered massage and brought her back to life. Waking up in the hospital, her first words were: "How did the match go?" Her boots and shinguards were ripped to shreds and set on fire. She had been deafened, but was otherwise expected to recover.

Mickey Capp, 47, was fishing off a pier in Deal, England, in early August when his rod glowed green "like a fluorescent tube" as lightning struck it. A shooting pain passed through his arms and chest and he dropped the rod. When he picked it up it happened again. He was probably saved from death by his rubber boots and the rod's plastic grip. Meanwhile, 50 miles away, his mother Gladys, 71, had just left her house in Southend, Essex, when lightning ripped through her living room and set the house on fire.

By September 10, five people had been killed in Britain 1994 by lightning, the highest toll for 10 years. EA Technology of Chester recorded 288,000 lightning ground strikes in July alone; the annual average is 300,000.

Nancy Wilde, 46, was with two friends at Windlesham Golf Club, near Sunningdale, England, on September 14 when she was struck by lightning on the fairway. Lars Oernfeldt, 20, a Danish-born St. John's Ambulance trainee, heard screaming and rushed to help. He opened Mrs. Wilde's mouth and smoke came out. She wasn't breathing and her hair was badly burned. He started heart massage and showed another man how to give mouth-to-mouth resuscitation. She stopped breathing several times. After about 10 minutes, an ambulance crew arrived. She had gone quite blue by the time they brought her back, and had been effectively dead for up to 10 minutes. She was expected to recover fully.

BABY JESUS RESURRECTED

Maria de la Conception, 30, five and a half months pregnant, went into labor on Christmas morning 1994. The baby was born at the Virgen de Rocio hospital in Seville, Spain, weighing only 1 pound 8 ounces. He was named Jesus at the suggestion of the midwife. Shortly afterwards, doctors announced that the baby had not survived.

The tiny body had been under refrigeration in the morgue for an hour and a half when the father, Feliciano Perejon, asked to take a last look and noticed the baby's chest move. "I just scooped him up and kissed him," said the 37-year-old electrician. "It was a miracle." Jesus was rushed to intensive care, but lost his fight for life three weeks later, on January 15.

In a related incident, a baby declared stillborn by doctors in Bhadrak, Orissa, India, on November 18, 1994, was dumped by the family in a field. The following morning, the baby was found alive and kicking with two stray dogs which had kept vigil through the night, and was taken to the hospital for attention.

STRANGE DEATHS

❦ Donald Tollett, 60, died from suffocation after a freak weather phenomenon called a stythe caused a drop in air pressure, sucking carbon dioxide from an unused coal mine. He was walking through the Karva Woodcrafts factory unit in Widdrington Station, Northumberland, England, on February 11, on his way to feed his niece's horse, accompanied by a family friend, David Wind, 8, and a pet dog when he and the collie were overcome.

❦ Renate Pancea died of carbon monoxide fumes which escaped after mice closed the chimney of his house in Mantua, Italy. Three of his relatives were also fatally gassed as they waited for a priest to read the last rites.

❦ A poacher electrocuting fish in a Polish lake died when he fell into the water and suffered the same fate as his quarry. The 24-year-old man was one of four who had attached a cable to a fishing net and a high-voltage electricity line.

❦ In an attempt to rescue a chicken on July 31, farmer's son Allam Sabet al-Sayyed, 18, descended a 60-foot well in the Egyptian village of Nazlat Imara, 240 miles south of Cairo. He drowned, apparently after an undercurrent in the water pulled him down. When he failed to appear, his brother Sayyed, 20, climbed down to investigate…and drowned. Then his brother Ahmad, 16, climbed down and vanished—to be followed by their 14-year-old sister, Zeinab. Two elderly cousins arrived to see if they could help, but suffered the same fate. The bodies of all six were later pulled out, along with the chicken, which was the only survivor.

❦ Three Fijian fishermen have recently choked to death on live fish. All three tried to kill their catch by biting its head. A fisherman from the island of Rabi was the first fatality last December. On January 14, a fish head lodged in the throat of Samueal Taoba, 50, from a village on the island of Vanua Levu. Its spines lodged in his gullet and he suffocated before his friends could pull it out. Serupepeli Lumelume, 22, died in exactly the same way on 14 February, while fishing in a river near Narvosa on the island of Viti Levu.

SAINT'S SEVERED HAND PROVIDES SUCCOR

Father John Kemble, a Catholic from Hereford, England, fell victim to the allegations of the blackguard and liar Titus Oates in 1678, and at the age of 79 was hanged for treason on Widemarsh Common. His left hand was hacked off by the executioner and saved by a woman in the crowd.

For nearly 200 years the hand has been carried round in its oak reliquary to the sick and those in need of spiritual succor. Kemble was one of the Forty Martyrs of England and Wales canonized by Pope Paul VI in 1970.

Father Christopher Jenkins, 63, a Benedictine monk and former headmaster of Belmont Abbey School, Hereford, has been acting for the last few months as parish priest at St. Francis Xavier's in Hereford, where St. John Kemble's naturally mummified hand has been kept in a shrine near the altar since 1806.

On July 15, Friar Jenkins had a severe stroke and doctors gave him little or no chance of recovery. His assistant, Friar Anthony Tumelty, took the hand to Hereford County Hospital and placed it on the comatose monk's head. From that time, friends say, he began to recover.

The hand of 17th-century saint John Kemble is thought to have healing powers.

"Nobody expected him to live," said Friar Tumelty, "but he came out of the coma within hours and is now walking, talking and eating. Even the doctors were surprised. It is not up to me to say whether his recovery is a miracle, but I must say that it is beyond our wildest hopes."

Dr. Thomas Stuttaford, writing in *The Times,* offers words of caution: "Apparent recovery in just over 24 hours after a stroke, even one that produced deep unconsciousness, is not uncommon."

CATS AND DOGS

❦ Russell and Pat Keeley reluctantly decided to have their 14-year-old tabby Sam put down when he became ill. Guy Lown, a vet, visited their home in Emmanuel Close in Suffolk, England, to give Sam an injection of sodium pentathol and declared him dead when his heart stopped beating. Mr. Keeley put the body in a box, but the next day, 17 hours after the injection, he opened the box for a last look only to see the cat's whiskers twitching. "He actually seems to have got better," he said. "He has started eating again and has had a whole rabbit in the last couple of days." The vet offered to give Sam another injection to finish him off, but Mr. Keeley, who refused to pay for the first injection, said: "There was no way we were going to have him put down again." Mr. Lown, of the Highcliff veterinary practice in Ipswich, said: "The dose we give is such an overdose that pets have no chance. I really don't know what happened. He went straight off to sleep after the injection, he had no ascertainable heartbeat at all and I was sure that was it, but I have seen him since he woke up and he now seems fairly well back to normal."

❦ Ze'ev and Haya Rotem from Rishon Lezion in Israel found that Donna, their 10-year-old basset hound, had a swollen foot. The local vet offered Ze'ev the choice of amputation or lethal injection. He chose the latter and returned an hour later to collect the body in a plastic bag. He buried his pet in a shallow grave in a nearby orchard. Six days later the Rotems returned home to discover Donna sleeping next to the house gate, alongside the family's other dog. Her paw seemed to have healed. The Rotems assumed that the injection had been insufficient to kill and that Donna had somehow managed to dig herself out of both plastic bag and grave.

❦ Another great survivor was Torver, an eight-year-old Yorkshire terrier. Charles and Muriel Leeming were convinced their pet had died when they saw him plunge off Clough Head peak in Helvellyn, England. Although his fall was twice broken by bushes, most of it was down an almost sheer slope of jagged scree. After a long and fruitless search, the Leemings returned home to Walley, Lancashire, convinced that Torver was dead; but their local vet, David Higginson, arranged for a local animal charity to distribute 50 posters and make local radio and newspaper appeals. After five days, the black and tan Yorkie was discovered, bedraggled and with a slight limp, beneath a camper four miles away.

❦ A dog was rescued from a collapsed two-story house in Kobe, Japan, 44 days after the Great Hanshin Earthquake of January 17, 1995. Kazuko and Yutaka Inui, both 63, escaped, but their 10-year-old dog Happy was trapped when her kennel was smashed by a falling wall. The couple returned several times to look for her, but when she didn't answer their calls they gave her up for dead. On March 2, as workers were removing debris, Happy staggered out, emaciated and too weak to make a sound. "She probably ate biscuits and other things we had at home," said Yutaka Inui. "We have no idea where she got water."

POLTERGEISTS

NEEDLES FROM NOWHERE

Bar staff at the Bull's Head Inn in Nuneaton, England, continue to be puzzled by the appearance of mystery needles in odd places—in shoes, on shelves, in bar mats, in the carpets, kitchen, curtains, etc.—often with bits of old, frayed cotton attached to them. A local writer discovered that Eliza Smith, a previous landlady who died in 1922, had been a highly respected seamstress. Recently, landlady Chris Leedham has noticed taps coming back on after being firmly turned off, a vibrating pub stool and a feeling of being watched. Barman Steve Higgot saw the apparition of a little old lady in her fifties walk from a side wall across the room to the end of the bar.

POLTERGEIST GIRL TRAGEDY

Some researchers firmly believe there is a connection between a troubled personality and the manifestation of paranormal phenomena or experiences, whether hoaxed or not. In March 1984, 14-year-old Tina Resch certainly fit the formula when she became the focus of a controversial poltergeist case in which, apparently by themselves, doors opened and shut, lights turned on and off and household objects flew across rooms in her home in her presence. The case came to light when eight members of her family had to flee the house in the North Side area of Columbus, Ohio.

Now aged 24, Tina has spent nearly three years in Carron County jail, charged with the murder of her two-year-old daughter Amber in 1992. The autopsy on Amber revealed injuries caused by physical assaults over a period of time. Also charged with her is her boyfriend of that time, David Herrin, 29. To avoid a possible death sentence, Tina has pleaded guilty although, through her lawyer, she claims she was at the home of a Carrollton woman who was helping her write a book about her earlier paranormal experiences.

Herrin, who seems to have been the last person to see Amber alive (when he put her to bed), has also attempted to avoid the death penalty by admitting sexual abuse of the child. Both blamed each other for the child's death and both were found guilty and jailed.

Tina's life had never been normal. When she was 10 months old, her mother carried her into the city's Children's Hospital, suffering from pneumonia, and never returned. She was adopted by John and Joan Resch into a household where there was a constant turnover of children. The Resches had fostered nearly 300 children over a 28-year period, who had come to them mentally or physically damaged by abuse or suffering from physical abnormalities. Tina became obsessed by the mystery of her parents' identities. At the time of the poltergeist outbreak, it was pointed out that she had seen the film *Poltergeist* several times, and closely identified herself with the boy hero who was plagued by objects that came to life in V. C. Andrews' novel *If There Be Thorns*.

As news of the Columbus poltergeist girl filled the news wires, her home was disrupted by endless visits from reporters, TV crews, paranormalists and, in the end, the skeptics led by James Randi. Randi was convinced the girl was hoaxing the activity and one TV cameraman appears to have caught Tina in the act of toppling a vase. However, Tina was championed by

William Roll, who runs the Psychical Research Foundation in North Carolina. For a while, Roll and Randi battled it out on a succession of talk shows and, as Tina's powers seemed to wane, eventually media interest subsided.

Tina married twice. Neither man was the father of Amber, but she retained their surnames, calling herself Tina Resch Bennett Boyer. Joan Resch, whose love gave Tina a safe if chaotic home, still stands by her in her latest ordeal. "I don't think she did it," says Joan. "Amber was all she had." Tina still maintains that most of the phenomena that happened 11 years ago were real, but that after all the publicity her life "became hell."

SEEING IS BELIEVING

❧ Betty Parker of Colorado spied on her neighbor Gary Clowes for six weeks. Every night, Clowes and his fellow cultists would dress up in "the robes of the devil," perform brutal human and animal sacrifices and shout unintelligible words. She persuaded members of her local church to break into Clowes's house armed with crosses, stakes and prayer books. It transpired that Clowes and his friends were rehearsing Shakespeare's *Julius Caesar*. (The "human and animal sacrifices" were the murder of Caesar and the ritual killing of a rubber chicken.)

❧ Pat Leigh was woken in the early hours at home in Marden, near Devizes, Wiltshire, England, by two phone calls. The first time she heard groaning and moaning and assumed it was an obscene call. When the telephone rang again, she heard more groaning and her 25-year-old daughter Amanda cry: "Oh my God!" Then she could hear a man's voice. Thinking that her daughter was being attacked, she rang the police, who rushed to her daughter's house. Amanda had been enjoying a night of passion with her boyfriend. It was presumed that one of them had twice unwittingly pressed the last-number redial button on the bedside telephone with a toe.

❧ There was a bomb scare at Manchester Airport in England after figures were seen on a security video placing a package by a hangar. They turned out to be night shift engineers staging a joke burial service, with a wreath-laying, for Mickey—a mouse that used to nibble their sandwiches.

❧ According to *Birding World* magazine, an excited announcement by an expert "twitcher" on CB radio led to birdwatchers flocking to his side in a field on the Isle of Scilly. Only when scores of telescopes were focused on the object of his attention was it realized that the nighthawk, a rare visitor from North America was in fact a cowpat.

❧ North Devon coast guards and an RAF Sea King helicopter scoured the sea off Putsborough Beach near Woolacombe, England, after reports that a skydiver had plunged into the sea. The rescuers found a five-foot-tall inflatable clown, origin unknown.

UFOs

JET IN NEAR MISS WITH UFO

A British Airways Boeing 737, on an evening flight from Milan on January 6, had a close encounter with something 17 minutes from touchdown at Manchester Ringway Airport in England. Captain Roger Wills and Flight Officer Mark Stuart ducked down in the cockpit when the brightly lit wedge-shaped craft appeared only yards in front of them at 13,000 feet over the Pennines. Air traffic control at Ringway told them that theirs was the only plane showing on radar. As they waited for the impact, they saw the UFO flash down the right-hand side of the aircraft and disappear.

The Boeing landed safely at 7 P.M., with the 600 passengers apparently unaware of the encounter. A detailed log and sketches were sent to the Joint Air Miss Working Group, part of the Civil Aviation Authority. The pilots refused to talk to the press, but one of their colleagues said "they are high-grade, sensible guys."

CHINESE UFOS

People in three different parts of Guangxi province in China claimed to have seen UFOs at the same time, according to the semiofficial China News Service. On the night of July 26, dozens of workers saw a UFO three meters in diameter, rising 1,500 to 2,000 meters from the ground just northwest of a coal mining area in Guangxi's Huanjiang county.

"The shape of the object was just like the sun perched on top of a crescent moon," the report said. "As it as-cended, the size of the object grew gradually smaller while its glow faded. After approximately seven minutes, it disappeared completely."

At about the same time, a government official in Tian'e county witnessed a "strange star" in the sky, saying it was about the same size as the moon. "Its glow was similar to that of the moon, but it did not shine towards the ground," the man said. The "strange star" then rose in the air and vanished after two minutes."

Meanwhile, residents of Yizhou prefecture and Locheng county reported seeing a similar object. They said it appeared "in the form of a silvery halo or a sun perched on top of a crescent moon" and shone like the lights of a car. The object soon disappeared.

OFFICIAL: ROSWELL PAPERS DESTROYED

Any hope that the U.S. Government's General Accounting Office (GAO) investigation into the administration of the Roswell Army Air Field (RAAF) might clear up the mystery of the alleged July 1947 UFO crash nearby has faded. Their report confirms that nearly all the base's administrative records and messages between March 1945 and December 1949 are missing, presumed destroyed.

Steve Schiff—the Republican congressman for New Mexico whose inquiries into the incident helped bring about the official investigation—said that while the RAAF was telling the world that the debris recovered from the crash site was nothing more than a weather balloon, the missing messages would have revealed what the Roswell military officials were telling their superiors. "It is my understanding that these outgoing messages were permanent records which should never have been destroyed," said Schiff. The GAO discovered that the documents were destroyed about 40 years ago, but not by whom or why.

The two documents successfully located refer to the wreckage as "a radar tracking device," but Schiff believes this to be part of the original "cover-up." While many UFO buffs will be disappointed by this low-level information which comes without any hint of re-

covered alien bodies, Schiff praised the GAO for their thoroughness. He said: "At least this effort caused the Air Force to acknowledge that the crashed vehicle was no weather balloon. That explanation never fit the fact of the high military secrecy used at the time."

A copy of the report—which admits that "the debate on what crashed at Roswell continues"—can be obtained by calling the GAO office in Washington (202) 513-6000 and asking for document number GAO/NSIAD-95-187.

CLOSE ENCOUNTERS & ALIEN ABDUCTIONS

BONNYBRIDGE GOES INTERGALACTIC

By the time you read this, the Earth may have its first alien ambassador. We don't mean the longed-for landing on the White House lawn, but a personal appearance of a representative of the Intergalactic Council of Nine at the town hall in Bonnybridge, the apparent epicenter of Scotland's three-year run of UFO activity.

Falkirk district councillor Billy Buchanan, who also holds a seat on the Central Regional Council at Sterling, says he has had a whole series of meetings with a black-suited being called Zal-us who materializes in Billy's office. Billy has managed to convince Zal-us that the time has come for the rest of Bonnybridge to see him too, so Billy has hired the local town hall for $60 so that Zal-us can make his maiden speech to earthlings on October 9.

"What this man has to say will be the most important thing we have ever heard," says Billy of this date with destiny. It seems Zal-us will be a big hit with the style mags and matrons, as he is described as a cross between a cosmic

Blues Brother and a Man-in-Black with Robert Redford's looks. "He has fair hair and looks almost Scandinavian," said Billy. "He has a weird look, both youthful and well-aged. There's something about his piercing blue eyes that seems to hold all the knowledge of the world."

Billy Buchanan has arranged a town meeting with Zal-us, the fair-haired alien.

These encyclopedic eyes saw right through Billy. "Much of my conversation with Zal-us was so technical that most of it went right over my head."

EERIE GLOW IN THE PACIFIC

In early June 1994, a fleet of yachts left New Zealand for Tonga, 1,500 miles to the northeast. About halfway there, a storm slammed into the fleet. Twelve yachts were abandoned while one, *Quartermaster,* with a crew of three, disappeared. The navy survey ship *Monowai* was approaching the sinking yacht *Ramtha* at about 4 A.M. on June 5 when crew members reported seeing a mysterious light.

Dramatic video footage showed perilous seas in which the ship rolled up to 48 degrees in enormous waves and darkness. Suddenly it all changed. "The sky just lit up and we could see for miles, it was really strange," said midshipman Tracy Kaio. On *Ramtha,* Bill Forbes found the deck all lit up. "Floating above us in low cloud was…a glowing mass of white light with just a tinge of orange."

Under the light was the 12-meter catamaran *Heart Light,* sailed by Americans Divinie and Darryl Wheeler and their two children. Divinie said the storm was supernatural. When the boat reached a point under the light she claimed it simply stopped and was caught in "a powerful tractor beam from a Seventh Realm spacecraft *[sic]*." She writes that it was *Heart Light's* destiny to be sunk at that spot. They tried to sink it before rescue but could not do so without killing themselves. Before they would agree to rescue by San Te Maru, the fishing boat skipper had to agree to sink it. The rescue was made and *Heart Light* was rammed and sunk—although, officially, New Zealand was told it broke up.

Some boats abandoned were later salvaged; as for the *Quartermaster,* only its empty life raft was found.

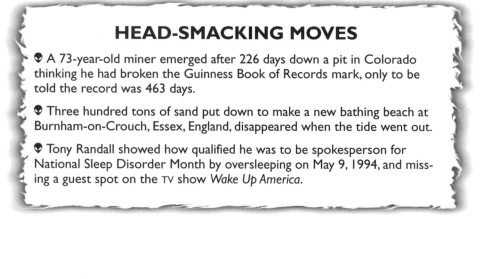

HEAD-SMACKING MOVES

❂ A 73-year-old miner emerged after 226 days down a pit in Colorado thinking he had broken the Guinness Book of Records mark, only to be told the record was 463 days.

❂ Three hundred tons of sand put down to make a new bathing beach at Burnham-on-Crouch, Essex, England, disappeared when the tide went out.

❂ Tony Randall showed how qualified he was to be spokesperson for National Sleep Disorder Month by oversleeping on May 9, 1994, and missing a guest spot on the TV show *Wake Up America.*

PARANORMAL EXPERIENCES

KANGAROO COURT

Sorcery is so rampant at Miami's county courthouse that an official "Voodoo Squad" has been established to clean up dead chickens, goats, charms and other remnants of ceremonies each morning. Many of the defendants on trial in Dade County are Cuban and Haitian natives. Relatives sometimes sneak into an empty courtroom and sprinkle voodoo powder on judges' benches and lawyers' chairs. In one case, two dead lizards, their mouths tied shut with twine, were found during a break in a cocaine trial. Other items commonly found on the courthouse grounds include corn kernels, which are supposed to speed up a trial date; eggs, which make a case collapse; cakes, which sweeten a judge's attitude towards a defendant; and black pepper, to keep someone jailed.

UNPINNING THE DRAGON

The true extent of the ancient Oriental belief in elemental forces was glimpsed during the March celebration in South Korea of the 50th anniversary of its liberation from Japanese occupation.

In a week-long operation near Andong in central South Korea, soldiers with mine detectors searched for metal stakes buried more than 50 years ago by the Japanese army in a war of intercultural magic intended to "disrupt Korean feng-shui earth energies," according to the Yonhap news agency.

During their rule from 1910 to 1945, Japanese governors ordered thousands of stakes to be driven into the ground at spots that were thought to be springs of the nation's life energy—

particularly sacred sites dedicated to local shamanic traditions. The policy had a lasting effect and although shamanism has survived in Korea, these days it is much diminished, a situation the Koreans are seeking to reverse.

CAB-NAPPER POSSESSED

An Indian man, arrested for stealing a taxi and kidnapping the driver, confessed to the charges, explaining that he had been cursed by an aunt in India: the ghost of an anonymous old woman periodically entered his body, causing him to do "bad things." His bouts of possession, he said, were preceded by a fog which drifted towards him, settled on his chest and entered his body through his nose and mouth.

Visits to exorcists in India failed to cure him. Psychiatrists Anthony Hale and Narasimha Pinninti diagnosed a "dissociative state of paranoid schizophrenia," but were disconcerted when the prison chaplain told them he had seen the ghost possess the patient in prison. He saw "a descending cloud" and, according to the psychiatrists, "an impression of a face alarmingly like a description of the dead woman given

PECULIAR PRESS

LOST TREES FOUND IN SCOTTISH HIGHLANDS
New Scientist, Aug. 6, 1994

29 HURT AS STUDENTS DEMAND RIGHT TO CHEAT
Canberra Times, Aug. 8, 1994

LAZY, FAT DRAGONS TO GO ON CRASH DIET IN ZOO
Bangkok Post, Aug. 9, 1994

to us by the patient." Similar reports came from frightened cellmates.

The patient was nonetheless treated with trifluoperazine and clopenthixol, which apparently "exorcised" the ghost. Hale and Pinninti concluded that "neuroleptics may relieve symptoms of exorcism-resistant possession." Later the patient was discharged and the "ghost" returned when he failed to take his medication.

PARANORMAL POWER THEFT

Fourteenth-century Heol Fanog House, near the Brecon Beacons in Wales, has plagued its occupants since they moved there in 1989. Self-employed artist Bill Rich, his wife, Liz, and children Ben (four), Rebecca (three) and Thomas (10 months), have endured smells of sulfur and church incense, as well as ghostly footsteps. One afternoon in 1990, a phantom figure walked past Mrs. Rich in the kitchen and disappeared into the wall. Occasionally they heard a noise like a cat snoring.

"Since we moved in," said Bill, "the electricity bills have been remarkable. We had one for $1,125 the first quarter we were here. Whatever it is also uses the electricity when all the appliances are off and even when we are away. We estimate that altogether we have had to pay for about $4,500 worth of electricity that we haven't used."

They also suffered ill effects. "The children would get wound up, though away from the house they were fine," said Bill. "Liz and I felt terribly weak, as if we'd just put in a shift on a building site."

The Riches brought in several exorcists to try and sort things out. A group of mediums for Cardiff's Spiritualist Church claimed to have expelled four ghosts; later, the Reverend David Holmwood toured the house and an-

nounced: "I've met a man who died at the end of the last century. He's been stuck in a thorn bush ever since."

A few days earlier, Bill had painted a picture of a man stuck in a thorn bush in response to a dream. After the priest blessed the house, the snoring cat departed, but ghostly figures continued to appear and Bill had to tape down the light switches to prevent them from being turned on in the night.

In March 1994, the house was visited by the medium Eddie Burks. Burks said he found the highest concentration of evil he had ever come across, and that it was feeding off electricity for its own power. It was also taking it from the family. Burks went into a trance and claimed to have drawn the power out of the property and into himself. The following month, the daily electricity costs fell from $7.50 to $3, and there were no more ghost sightings.

The family applied to SWALEC, the local electricity board, for a $4,500 rebate. The board had already rewired the house and installed four test meters, but had been unable to detect any abnormal fluctuation. At the time of the last report, the rebate was not forthcoming and the Riches were still looking for another house.

HOODOO THAT VOODOO

In March 1994, Beverly Johnson from Arcadia, Louisiana, was suffering headaches that wouldn't respond to medication. One report mentions "family tension." Her father, Chester Crawford, suggested she see a man called Benny, described as a hoodoo man. Hoodoo is a Black American faith that combines elements of Haitian voodoo with Biblical verse and Catholicism.

Benny said that Beverly, 35, was under attack by demons who were trying to possess her. On the advice of Chester, Beverly and her two younger sisters, Doretha Crawford, 34, and Myra Obasi, 30, fled with their five children from Arcadia, a remote, pine-forested town of about 3,000 people, making for the home of another sister in Dallas, Texas, 200 miles away. Reports do not make clear why all three sisters felt threatened.

Less than an hour later, on Interstate 20, thinking their car was hexed, they dumped it and rented another at Shreveport airport. After checking into a motel in Tyler, Texas, the children started seeing things. The sisters then piled into the car and drove to Mar-shall, where they found a house with a cross in front of it and left the children at the door. They were eventually returned to the family.

Myra, an elementary school teacher, drove on towards Dallas with her sisters in the early hours of March 18. Suddenly, Myra attempted to veer the car into the path of oncoming traffic and off the sides of bridges. Then the steering wheel appeared to squirm into life and started to pummel her, before mutating into a monstrous demon. The apparition sprang from the dashboard and possessed her. "Her whole features

ARCHIVE GEMS

THE HAND OF GOD

Something celestial fell from the sky and panicked the residents of Bakersville in June 1914. The mysterious object was shaped like a malformed hand and emitted "a great white light" as it plummeted on to the farm of Henry Prantl. When recovered hours later, it was still "sizzling" hot and described as "resembling a hand of a human burned off at the wrist. The "thumb" and "little finger" are unusually long and there are "nails" on some of the fingers.

The event created a sensation among the superstitious of the neighborhood, who believed it to be connected with the death of Prantl's son Randolph the previous month, about which the report of the "flaming hand," as it came to be called in the *Niagara Falls Gazette* (June 6, 1914) tells us no more.

The report is also frustratingly brief and vague on the salient facts. "Scientists" were said to be baffled and yet identified the object as "part of a shooting star." It is clearly not a conventional meteor. It was not composed of iron but some light material "different from any other meteoric compositions seen in this part of the world."

The shape of the object is distinctly unconventional and one has to wonder how it survived the impact. Indeed, it might not be meteoric at all, but an actual instance of that phenomenon by which the 19th-century astronomer Leverrier explained away true meteorites: he claimed they were in the ground all the time and were only revealed when they were struck by lightning. Lightning striking certain kinds of soil or sand can actually fuse the material along its branching path, creating objects called fulgurites which look remarkably like this "flaming hand."

But if the "hand" is a fulgurite, how did it stay hot for so long and what was the nature of the extraordinary light which attracted the attention of searchers in the first place? It is difficult to tell after such a lapse of time.

LOVE HURTS

❤ When Iraq attacked Israel during the Gulf War, one of those to suffer was a wife whose cache of passionate letters and intimate pictures of her lover were uncovered when a Scud missile demolished her home. They were found by her husband as he sifted through the rubble. He filed for divorce.

❤ Unnamed, embarrassed, and in great pain, a middle-aged man turned up at the fire station in December 1987 with a belt-buckle stuck on his manhood. It became stuck during sex games with his wife at their home in Bristol, England, and after three hours of tugging at it he asked his son to drive him to the fire station. He arrived with a shopping bag packed with ice wrapped around his member, which by then was badly swollen and turning black. The firemen, unfortunately, were unable to help, and he was taken to Bristol Royal Infirmary, where he was eventually set free by doctors.

❤ Charnchai Puanmuangpak was 13 years old and addicted to the Thai perversion known as "pumping." Most pumpers use a bicycle pump, inserting the nozzle into their rectum and giving themselves a rush of air, but Charnchai decided to go further. He moved on to a two-cylinder foot-pump and then, egged on by schoolfriends, decided he was going to try the compressed air hose at a nearby gas station. One evening in August 1993 he sneaked in to the station. Not realizing how powerful the machine was, he inserted the tube into his body, put a coin in the slot, and was killed almost instantly.

changed," said Doretha. "She spoke in a man's voice. Mist came out of her mouth. Her teeth were black and scattered. It wasn't her. It said it had got her and it was going to get us too."

The three terrified women abandoned the car in Waxahachie, 30 miles south of Dallas, and hitched a ride with a truck closer into the city. They were directed to the house of Maddy Bradfield, an elderly preacher. An onlooker, Legayla Jones, watched the sisters shout and pray for about seven hours before they pushed garlic into Myra's eyes and paper down her throat. Myra, whose face looked strange with red, bulging eyes, offered no resistance. Confusingly, Bradfield later told the Dallas police that Myra was possessed by the demonic spirit of her father.

At some point Myra's eyeballs were gouged out with something sharp, possibly fingernails, and left in a waste bin. All three sisters claim not to remember how this happened; they thought the demon or Satan himself was to blame. Doctors in the Parkland Memorial Hospital in Dallas said that whoever removed the eyes—termed "bilateral enucleation" on her admission sheet—did it with clinical precision.

Detectives were unable to question Myra for several hours because she was chanting "Thank you, Jesus" continuously. She refused to press charges against her sisters, but in September they were convicted of aggravated assault and sentenced to 10 years' probation.

According to hoodoo lore, when a person becomes possessed by a spirit, he or she becomes the spirit's horse. To rid the person of the spirit you either cut the head off or gouge the eyes out. A blinded horse is no use, so the spirit leaves.

There was a curious echo of this tale at the beginning of 1994. A 26-year-old man from Merriam, Kansas, looked in the mirror and saw a pentagram in his right eyeball. Interpreting this as a sinister occult symbol, he popped the eyeball out, cut the connecting tendons with a kitchen knife and flushed it down the lavatory.

A year earlier, Bernadette French, 36, a manic depressive who gouged her eyes out in Wilmington Hospital, Delaware, was awarded $1.1 million after contending that hospital staff didn't supervise her properly.

BRIGHT SPARK

A boy of 10 is the latest example of an "Electric Person." Liam Lowsley of Bransholme, England, relishes being the center of attention at school as blue sparks fly off his arms and legs when anyone comes close to him. It has its downside too: he cannot operate the class computer and the sparking sensation is unpleasant. He says: "It's worse than pins and needles."

Schoolboy Liam Lowsley is a pint-sized power plant.

Professor Don Whitehead, head of electrical engineering at Hull University, explained that as Liam moves about he is generating huge charges of static electricity. "It is almost certainly to do with the clothes or shoes Liam wears, combined with the dry atmosphere," he said. The phenomenon seems to happen only at Liam's school, where considered opinion relates its onset to a severe thunderstorm the previous month when the building was struck by lightning. Teacher Jonathan Roe said: "We think the scaffolding around the school may be acting as a conductor."

AUTO-REVERSE

Pam Lucas of North Hill, Fareham, in England had an electricity man come to fix her cooker on May 30. "I was looking out of the window when smoke started pouring from his van," she said. "Then it just leapt forward a few feet and hit our house."

Firemen had the blaze under control before the house was badly damaged. The engine and cab were gutted. An electrical fault was thought to have started the van up, even though there were no keys in the ignition.

In late July, a motorist in Clair Park, Haywards Heath, got the fright of his life when the driverless parked car in front of him started up, reversed into him and burst into flames. Firemen believed there had been a short circuit in the ignition system, and the car jumped backwards because the owner had left it in reverse.

THE FACES OF BELMEZ

Thousands of faces have appeared and disappeared over the years in the concrete floor of a home in Belmez de la Moraleda, a remote village in southern Spain, according to its 75-year-old owner, Maria Gomez Pereira.

The widow has lived with the enigmatic figures for 24 years since the first one appeared on the hearthstone of her fireplace on August 23, 1971. Unable to scrub away the image, she had the entire hearth covered with an inch of cement—but the same picture reappeared on its surface. When further faces appeared on the stones of the fireplace, the news spread and soon the house was besieged by journalists, investigators and curiosity-seekers.

The hearthstone was raised and hung on the wall. Maria, her husband and two sons charged people 25 cents to see it. When the earth beneath was excavated, human bones were allegedly found about nine feet down. Villagers speculated that the faces were caused by restless spirits from an ancient graveyard beneath the house. Soon, 20 or more images covered the floors. Some faded away after a few hours, to be replaced by new ones. Professor German de Argumosa, a paranormal investigator, believed a poltergeist was responsible. He kept watch for many days and claimed to witness the faces as they appeared.

Analysis of the pictures showed they contained zinc, copper, chrome, phosphorus, lead and barium. There was no evidence of paint. Investigators left tape recorders in the room and picked up strange voices—heavy breathing, whimperings of small children and a quarrel. A woman's voice shouted: "Drunkard! I don't want drunkards in here!" and a man replied: "Go in, woman, go in...I don't want...My God!"

At Easter in 1972, vast crowds jammed the streets of the village. Then, on April 3, 1975, *The Sun* newspaper claimed that the whole phenomenon had been a hoax by the 2,103 villagers, using "trick photography" to encourage tourism. This sounded as far-fetched as the phenomenon itself. Scientists have shown that the outlines are not painted or drawn. "Experts have taken pieces away to analyze in Madrid and Valencia," she said, "but they couldn't say what it was."

The present mayor, Paco Donato Hervas, said: "People now accept there's no explanation. But there are some who say that when Maria dies there will be no more faces. We get carloads of visitors, sometimes even a busful. They just go to the house, look at the faces and often leave without even stopping for a drink. The village doesn't make money out of this, nor does Maria—although she has charged newspapers and television to take pictures."

Professor Felix Ares de Blas, who has studied the faces for several years, said recently: "It's possible that they were caused by acid or by silver nitrate, which would have turned the cement darker in places." Cesar Tort, a Mexican investigator, has taken up this hypothesis in *The Skeptical Inquirer*, suggesting that the motive was profit. Mrs. Pereira and her family were reported to have made $2,000 from charging the public to see the faces in the year after they were discovered. Up to 1,000 people a day visited the house before the mayor put a stop to the trade.

SOURCES

SOURCES

THE HUMAN WORLD

Antiquities 4

Praise Him from Whom All Shorthand Flows: *Times* (London), Aug. 6, 1994.

Prophylactic Tactics: *Daily Record*, Sept. 28, 1993.

Well of Hope: *Sheppey Gazette*, Oct. 6, 1993; *Woman's Own*, Dec. 20, 1993; *Adscene*, June 2, 1995.

Holy Grail Taken for a Spin: *Guardian*, June 20, 1994; *Times*, June 21, 1994.

It's About Time: *Daily Record*, June 25, 1994; *Laurence* (MA) *Eagle Tribune*, Oct. 4, 1994; *[Associated Press]*, March 17, 1995; *[Reuters]*, Sept. 22, 1994.

Tree Tribes Charted: *[Agence France Press]*, Aug. 15, 1995; *[AP]*, Sept. 11, 1995; *Guardian*, Sept. 14, 1995.

Say What?: *Guardian*, July 20, 1994; *Sunday Mail*, June 26, 1994; *Daily Telegraph*, Aug. 8, 1995; *[R]*, Aug. 10, 1995.

Strange Behavior 7

Mower Odyssey: *[AP]*, Aug. 25, 1994.

Windsurfing to Freedom: *[AFP]*, Feb. 11, 1994.

Explosive Footwear: *Daily Yomiuri*, Sept. 6, 1995.

Criminals Nail Themselves: *[R]*, Aug. 6, 1994.

Travel Mishaps: *[AP]*, Jan. 5, 1995; *The European*, Nov. 18, 1994; *Los Angeles Times*, July 10, 1994.

Tummy Rumbles: unavailable.

Stump Fever: *Victoria* (BC) *Times-Colonist*, May 20, 1994; *Scotsman*, May 26, 1994; *Star*, June 3, 1994.

Love Hurts: *Western Morning News*, Aug 3, 1994; *Halifax Eve. Gazette*, Aug. 15, 1994; *D. Star*, Sept. 13, 1994; *Guardian*, July 25, 1994.

Cultural Curiosities: *[AFP]*, Sept. 12,

1994; *Edinburgh Eve. News*, March 20, 1995; *Guardian*, Dec. 14, 1994; *Daily Mail*, Nov. 12, 1994; *Daily Star*, Aug. 1, 1994.

Out with a Bang: *Rocky Mountain News*, Aug. 14, 1994.

Sweet Smell of Self-Immolation: *[AP]*, Sept. 1, 1994.

Sons of Bitches: Boys Raised by Dogs: *Times*, Dec. 16, 1994; *Daily Mail*, Dec. 17, 1994; *[R]*, July 14, 1994; *Daily Mirror*, March 18, 19, 23, 24; *Daily Mail*, March 19, 1988; *[AP]*, March 18, 1990; *National Enquirer*, April 10, 1990; *Times, Daily Mirror, Daily Mail*, Nov. 20, 1992; *Daily Mirror, Daily Star*, May 26, 27, 1994; *People*, June 12, 1994.

Strange Death Schwascar: *Daily Star*, May 19, 1994; *N.Y. Post*, Oct. 27, 1994; *Daily Star*, June 25, 1994; *Daily Mail*, Nov. 17, 1994; *Daily Record*, Aug. 31, 1994; *Daily Record* (Scotland), Oct. 21, 1994; *[AP]*, Aug. 22, 1994; *[AP]*, Oct. 12, 1994.

Corpse Stolen in Dallas: *Daily Mirror*, Dec. 15, 1994; *Rocky Mountain News*, Dec. 15, 17, 1994.

Custom Coffin Case: *Manchester Metro News*, April 14, 21, 1995.

Wedding Dress Mystery: *Liverpool Echo*, April 4, 1995.

The Cavewoman of Cyprus: *Guardian*, May 23, 1995; *Independent*, May 25, 28, 1995; *Today*, May 27, 1995; *Observer*, May 28, 1995; June 11, 1995.

Legal Lunacy: *Kitchener* (Ontario) *Record*, Nov. 23, 1994; *Daily Telegraph*, March 17, 1995; *Sunday Mail*, Sept. 25, 1994; *N.Y. Post*, Sept. 2, 1994.

Vampire Wannabe: *Post*, Feb. 21, 1995; *Daily Mirror*, Feb. 22, 1995.

Twisted Dudes: *People*, Jan. 30, 1994; *Daily Mail*, March 28, 1995; *[AP]*, April 22, 1995; *[R]*, Sept. 22, 1994.

Identity Crisis: *Western Mail*, July 2, 1994.

133

Cults and Conspiracies 17

Postman Pat is a Digital Gangster: *Daily Mail, Daily Mirror,* Sept. 30, 1994.

You Can't Be Sirius: *Toronto Globe and Mail,* Nov. 19, 1994.

Pork-Poisoned Ammo: *Nazarene News Service,* July 2, 1993.

Kurt Cobain's Suicide Machine: *New Musical Express,* July 1, 1995.

Worldwide Weirdness: *[AP],* Nov. 28, 1994; *Times,* July 23, 1994; Telegraph, Sept. 14, 1994; *[AFP],* Sept. 22, 1994; *[AFP],* Aug. 15, 1994.

Deaths and Suicides 19

Poet Judged a Poor Cover: Rheinpfalz, March 23, 1994.

Pickled Stiff Gets Earthed: *[AP],* June 26, Aug. 6, 1994.

Lost and Found: *D. Star,* July 19, 1994; *Overseas Jobs Express,* Aug. 15, 1993.

Requiem for Dr. Lobotomy: unavailable.

Free-Fall Foul-Up: unavailable.

Freeze-Framed: *Daily Record, Daily Telegraph, Independent,* Dec. 24, 1994.

Maniac Surgeon: *Bild,* Nov. 8, 1994.

What's In a Name?: *Ivoir'Soir* (Ivory Coast), April 21, 1994; *Guardian,* Sept. 2, 1993, Feb. 10, 1994; *Times,* July 14, 1994; *Sunday Mail,* June 13, 1993; *Winston-Salem Journal,* July 2, 1993; *Daily Mirror,* June 18, 1994; *Metronews* (Birmingham), Aug. 4, 1994.

Genius and Discovery 23

And Robot Begot Robot: *[R],* July 21, 1994.

Hasn't Learned About Rounding Up: *China Daily,* April 22, 1995.

Severed Souvenirs: Elvis's Wart and Einstein's Brain: *Guardian,* Dec. 17, 1994; Arena "Relics," BBC-TV, April 1, 1994.

Twisted Dudes: *Wolverhampton Express & Star,* Oct. 5, 1994; *USA Today,* Jan. 28, 1994; *N.Y. Post,* Dec. 21, 1994.

So That's What They Do Between Customers: *Bangkok Post,* July 9, 1994.

Hoaxes and Panics 25

Head Cases: *The Times,* July 23, 1994.

That Ain't No Lady: *Ogden* (UT) *Standard Examiner,* July 12-21, 1995; *Meriden* (CT) *Record Journal,* July 14, 1995; *[AP],* July 14, 1995.

Foolish Felon Schwascar: *[R],* Nov. 5, 1993; *Daily Star,* Nov. 2, 1994; *[AP],* Sept. 8, 1994; *Kitchener* (Ontario) *Record,* Jan 7, 1995; *Daily Telegraph,* Aug. 27, 1994; *Daily Telegraph,* March 3, 1994; *Daily Telegraph,* Dec. 5, 1994.

The Goblin of Cheddar: *Bournemouth Advertiser,* Feb. 2-March 2, 1995.

Cannibal Courses: *Europa Times,* Jan. 1994; *Wolverhampton Express & Star,* June 1, 1994; *Today,* June 2, 1994; *[R],* April 8, 1994.

Strange Deaths: *Guardian Western Mail,* July 10, 1995; *Times,* July 12, 1995; *[AP],* Feb. 3, 1995; *Sunday Express,* April 23, 1995; *Sunday Express,* May 14, 1995; *Daily Mirror,* May 19, 1995.

Mupore Messiah: *The Monitor* (Uganda), Sept. 30-Oct. 3, 1994.

Archive Gems: Illinois Enema Bandit *[AP],* April 5, 1975; Correspondence with John Finley, April 5, 1975.

Ineptitude and Stupidity 30

Killed While Showing Cheek: *Sun,* Nov. 22, 1994.

Purposeful Priest Puncher: *Daily Star,* June 7, 1993.

Little Devils: *Daily Yomiuri,* Feb. 16, 1994.

Truly, the Pitts: *Daily Telegraph,* Sept. 9, 17, 1994; *Guardian,* Sept. 17, 1994.

Lethal Loyalties: *Burlington Free Press,* July 1, 1994.

Stubborn Bastard: *[AP],* Feb. 10, 1993; *[R],* Dec. 6, 1994.

Nut Cases: *N.Y. Post,* Nov. 17, 1994; *Victoria Times-Colonist,* Nov. 24, 1994; *Cincinnati Enquirer,* Oct. 9, 11, 30, 1994; *N.Y. Post, N.Y. Daily News,* March 17, 1994; *People,* Oct. 3, 1993.

THE ANIMAL WORLD

Out-of-Place Animals   36

Let Your Fingers Find the Falcon: *Derby Eve. Telegraph,* Feb. 10, 1995.
Camel Clean: *People,* Jan. 9, 1994.
Golfer Hooks Monster Pike: *Daily Mail, Daily Telegraph,* Feb. 22, 1995.
Gator Gawking: *Star,* July 22, 1994.
Spiders Colonize Hampstead: *Evening Standard,* Oct. 5, 1994; *Big Issue,* Aug. 9, 1994.
Where Did I Put Those Penguins?: *Daily Telegraph,* Jan. 7, 1995; *Wolverhampton Express & Star,* Dec. 9, 1994; *[AP],* Jan. 20, 1995; *Brisbane Courier Mail,* July 9, 1994; *Teddington & Hampton Times,* April 22, 1994; *Manchester Metro News,* June 10, 1994; *The Times,* Dec. 2, 1994; *Big Issue,* Dec. 5, 1994; *[R],* July 20, 1994; *Daily Telegraph,* Aug. 27, Sept. 12, 1994.
Animal Suicide Schwascar: *China Daily,* July 16, 1994; *[AFP],* July 13, 1994; *Bangkok Post,* Feb. 18, 1994; *[AP],* Jan. 5, 1995; *[AP],* April 12, 1994.
Crab Hitches Ride with Seagull: *Brighton Eve. Argus,* Oct. 6, 1994.
Bachelor Bird: *Edinburgh Eve News,* April 5, 1995
Coin-Carrying Cod: *Sun, Star,* June 15, 1994.

Attacks by Animals   40

Killer Worms Slobber on South: *Western Daily Press,* April 15, 1994; *Newcastle Journal,* April 15-16, 1994: *Guardian,* April 19-28, 1994; *New Scientist,* June 18, 1994.
Deranged by Dodgy Anchovies: *[AP],* July 11, 1995; *New Scientist,* July 22, 1995; *Independent,* July 24, 1995.
New York's Wildlife: *N.Y. Post,* Feb. 9, 1995; *N.Y. Times, N.Y. Daily News,* Feb. 17-21, 1995; *N.Y. Newsday,* Feb. 20, 1995; *N.Y. Post,* May 24, 1995;
Denver Post, June 2, 1995; *Observer,* June 18, 1995.
Love Hurts: *Daily Star,* Jan. 12, 1995; *Sunday Express,* July 26, 1987; *Western Mail,* Nov. 8, 1989.
Rest in Beast: unavailable.
Midnight Creepers: *Daily Mail,* Feb. 16, 1995.
Expensive Tastes: *People,* June 6, 1993.
Delinquent Dolphins: *Scotsman,* Nov. 14, 1994; *Observer,* Dec. 4, 1994; *[R],* Dec. 10, 12, 1994.
Beware of Beasts: *Sunday Times,* July 9, 1995; *Times of Malta,* Jan. 25, 1995; *Guardian,* Jan. 27, 1995; *[AP],* July 22, 1994; *Ivoir'Soir* (Ivory Coast), Feb. 14, 1995.
Animal Saboteurs: *[AP],* June 3-July 11, 1995; *South China Morning Post,* Nov. 10, 1994; *Ivoir'Soir* (Ivory Coast), Feb. 14, 1995; *Sussex Eve. Argus,* Oct. 29, 1994: *Brisbane Sunday Mail,* Dec. 11, 1994.
Death on the Hoof: *[AFP],* June 24, 1994.
Bovine Betrothal?: *[AFP],* March 2, 1995.
Foxy Hounds Hounded: *Daily Mirror, Sun,* Feb. 21, 1995.
Pooper Scooped: unavailable.

Attacks on Animals   46

Birds Dine On Birds: *[R],* Oct. 10, 1994; *Daily Mail,* Nov. 12, 1994.
Strange Deaths: *[R],* Feb. 25, 1995; *Rocky Mountain News,* Sept. 10, 1994; *[AP],* Jan. 7, 1995; *[R],* Jan. 19, 1995.
Pulseless Pet: *Bangkok Post,* April 4, 1994
Hole in One: *Daily Telegraph, Sun, Daily Mirror,* June 2, 1995.
Rabid Russian: *[R],* Feb. 14, 1994.
Archive Gems: It's Raining Whale Blubber: unavailable.

Swarmings   49

Bees Pay Last Respects: *South Shropshire Journal,* June 24, 1994; *[R],* Sept. 8, 1994.

Sickly Critters: *[AP]*, Aug. 10–Sept. 7, 1994; *[R]*, July 14, 1995; *[AP]*, June 30, 1994; *Chuck Shepherd's News of the Weird*, April 8, 1994.

Animal Sabotage Schwascar: *Ivoir'Soir*, April 7, 1993; *Western Mail*, April 19, 1994; *Wolverhampton Express & Star*, Aug. 25, 1993; *Daily Telegraph*, Nov. 11, 1993; *Guardian*, Aug. 4, 1994; *Canberra Times*, Feb. 4, 1994; *[AP]*, May 13, 1994; *Guardian*, May 19, 1994.

New Species Found 51

Killer Sponge: *D. Telegraph*, Jan. 26, 1995.

Two Luvars Caught: *Guardian*, June 30, 1994; *Daily Mail*, July 1, 1994; *The Cornishman*, Aug. 4, 1994.

Hermaphrogoat: unavailable.

Animal Affections: In a Snailspin: *Harborne Gazette*, Aug. 1994; The Rat Sat on the Cat: *Edinburgh Eve. News*, April 25, 1995.

Tasmanian Tiger Sighting: *Sydney Morning Herald, Brisbane Courier Mail*, Jan. 30, 1995.

Return of the Woolly Jumper: *NY Times*, March 14, 1995.

Nuking the Poodle: *Halifax Eve. Courier*, Sept. 8, 1994; *Western Morning News*, Oct. 19, 1985; *Daily Mirror*, Dec. 13, 1990; *Daily Star*, June 11, 1992; *Shropshire Star*, Oct. 2-3, 1991.

New Mammal in 'Nam: *Guardian*, June 24, Aug.13, 1995.

Animal Anomalies: *Wall Street Journal*, Feb. 17, 1995; *Queensland Sunday Mail*, May 15, 1994; *New Scientist*, Dec. 17, 1994; *[AFP]*, June 29, 1995.

Terrible Termites: *Western Daily Press*, Oct. 28, 1994; *New Scientists*, Nov. 12, 1994; *[AFP]*, March 7, 1995; *Canberra Times*, March 12, 1995.

Shrimply Unbelievable: *Daily Express*, July 29, 1994; *Northern Echo*, May 12, 1994; *Daily Telegraph, Guardian*, May 13, 1994; *Newcastle Journal*,

May 18, 1994; *Chicago Sun-Times*, June 17, 1993; *Daily Telegraph*, Oct 7, 1993.

Misplaced Animal Parts: *Times*, July 18, 1995; *Western Australian*, June 29, 1994; *[R]*, Sept. 3, 1994; *Flight International*, Jan. 4-10, 1995; *Sun*, June 25, 1993; *Bristol Eve. Post*, Aug. 25, 1994; unavailable.

Demented Animal Attack Schwascar: *Independent on Sunday*, Canberra *Times*, March 12, 1995; *Press Trust of India*, March 31, 1995; *Toronto Globe and Mail*, Nov. 5, 1994; *[R]*, Feb. 2, 1995; *Sun*, Nov. 18, 1994; *Sunday Mail*, Dec. 4, 1994; *Sunday Express*, Dec. 11, 1994; *Daily Star*, July 29, 1994.

Mass Deaths 53

Porpoise Pile-Up: *New Scientist*, Oct. 15, 1994.

Lambs to the Slaughter: *Daily Yomiuri* (Japan), *Le Matin* (Benin), Aug. 4, 1995.

Manimals 59

China's Wildman: *[AP]*, Oct. 28, 1994; *China Daily*, Oct. 29, 1994; *Brisbane* (Aust.) *Sunday Mail*, Jan 8, 1995; *Times*, April 8, 1995; *Bangkok Post*, April 12, 1995; *[AFP]*, May 18, 1994; *[United Press International]*, July 12, 1995.

Malaysia's Bigfoot: *Scripps Howard News Service*, Jan. 13, 1995.

Looking Good in Them Genes: *Hong Kong Standard*, Jan. 8, 1995; *Halifax Eve. Courier*, Sept. 17, 1994; *Eastern Daily Press*, Sept. 17, 1994; *Sussex Express*, Sept. 23, 1994; *Victoria* (BC) *Times Colonist, Rocky Mountain News*, March 9, 1995; *[AFP]*, March 14; April 5, 1995; *Jerusalem Post*, June 10, 1995.

Sumatra's Shy Apeman: *Hong Kong Eastern Express*, Dec. 12, 1994; *Western Daily Press*, Feb. 22, 1995; *Guardian*, March 6, 1995; *Saga*, April 1995

Pakistan's Big Hairy One: *[AFP], Indonesian Sunday Times,* May 8, 1994.
Mystery Footprints in Borneo: unavailable.

Water Monsters   62

Morgawr is Back: *Falmouth Packet,* Aug. 17, 1995; *West Briton,* Sept. 12, 13, 14, 1995; *Western Morning News,* Sept. 13, 1995.
Mega-Beaver on the Loose: *[AP],* March 26, 1994.
Teggie and other Beasts of Bala: *Western Mail,* March 10, 1995; *Sunday Telegraph,* March 26, 1995; *Western Morning News,* April 4, 1995; *Liverpool Echo,* April 7, 1995.
The Congleton "Croc": *Congleton Chronicle,* June 2, 1995; *Living Wonders* by Michell & Rickard, 1982, p. 56.
Lovesick Grouper: *San Jose* (CA) *Mercury News,* Sept. 7, 1994.
Pacific Monster Sighted: *Victoria* (BC) *Time Colonist,* Sept. 29, 1994.

....

THE NATURAL
WORLD
....

Disasters, Natural & Man-Made 68

Barbecued Bacon in Hamm: *Daily Mirror,* July 21, 1995; *Sussex Eve. Argus,* July 25, 1995.
Lime-Basted: *Independent on Sunday,* July 10, 1994.
Paratrooping Redbacks: *Brisbane Courier Mail,* Sept. 24, 1995.
Drought, Fire and Haze: *[R],* Oct. 2-5, 1994.
Toddler Floats in Fiery Flood: *[AP, AFP],* Nov. 3-10, 1994.

Biological and Medical   69

Misassembled Man: *Northern Echo,* Sept. 14, 1995.
Commando Gets "Miracle" Hand Relief in the Jungle: *Eve. Standard,* Oct.

10, 1994; *Times, Guardian, Daily Telegraph, Western Morning News,* Oct. 11, 1994.
Summer's Bastard: *Western Daily Press,* July 13, 19, 1994; *Daily Mail,* July 13, 1994; *Birmingham Sunday Mercury,* Sept. 4, 1994; *The Times,* July 22, 1994.
Jurassic Bark: *[AP],* Dec. 14, 15, 1994.
Trees Groove to Radio Waves: *Daily Telegraph,* Jan. 12, 1995; *New Scientist,* Jan. 14, 1995.
Sydney Teenager Turns into Radio: *[Australian Associated Press],* Dec. 10, 1994.
See You in 95, Bro: *[AP],* Jan. 19, 1995.
Multi-Ethnic Family: *Daily Telegraph, Daily Mail,* Aug. 25, 1994.
Doubled-Wombed Wondergirls: *[AP],* Oct. 13, 1994; *[AP],* June 18, 1993.
Archive Gems: Uncombable Hair Syndrome: unavailable.
Urine Luck!: *Victoria* (BC) *Monday Magazine,* Dec. 3, 1992; *New Scientist,* Feb. 29, April 4, 1992; *Guardian,* Oct. 22, 1994; *Independent, Daily Telegraph,* April 11, 1995.
Free-Fall Fiasco Schwascar: *[AP],* Sept. 5, 1994; *Canadian Press,* Sept. 6, 1994; *Daily Mail, Daily Mirror,* Jan. 13, 1995; *Daily Telegraph,* Jan. 23, 1995; *Daily Telegraph,* April 4, 1994; *Guardian,* April 5, 1994; *Guardian,* June 29, 1994; *Daily Mail,* July 2, 1994.
Why Women Woo Whoppers: *The Scotsman,* Aug. 17, 1994.
Forever Amber: *Independent,* May 19, 1995; *New Scientist,* May 27, 1995.
Hum Misty for Me: *Daily Telegraph,* April 28, 1995; *New Scientist,* April 29, 1995.

Epidemics and Illness   77

Bubonic Plague Plot Foiled: *[AP],* May 17, 1995; *Austin* (TX) *America Statesman,* May 28, 1995.
Freakish Fertilizer: *[R, AP],* April 27, 1994.
Love Hurts: *Wolverhampton Express &*

Reporter (Malaga), July; *The Enter-tainer* (Costa del Sol), July 28, Aug. 3, 1994; *Newcastle Herald,* March 22, 1994; *Canberra Times,* Feb. 26, 1995; *[AP],* March 6, 1995; *Independent,* March 7, 1995.

Geophysical Activity   91
Loud Cleaners: *Hong Kong Standard,* Jan. 18, 1994.
Heavy Groceries: *Guardian,* June 11, 1994.
Earthquake Flattens Settlement: un-available.
Grandma Mullberry Parts the Waves: *[AP],* April 18, 1995.
Gold Spew: *N.Y. Times,* Oct. 28, 1994.
Disaster Potpourri in Papua New Guinea: *[Agencies],* Sept. 19-27, 1994.

THE
PARANORMAL
WORLD

Psychical Phenomena   96
Ancient Egyptian in Custody Battle: *Daily Telegraph,* March 2, 1995.
Lawyers Gag Barbie: *New Zealand Sun-day Star-Times,* June 5, 1994; *Times,* Aug. 31, 1994.
PIS-sed Off : *[AP],* May 22, 1995.
Wayward Travels: *The Times of Malta,* Jan. 31, 1994; *Western Morning News, Eastern Express* (Hong Kong), April 28, 1994; *Western Morning News, Bangkok Post,* June 29, 1994; *Poli-tiken* (Denmark), July 3, 1994; *West-ern Mail,* July 22, 1994.
Ingela's Night Mare: *Expressen,* Aug. 22, 1995.
The Seoul Survivors: *[AP],* July 10, 12, 1995; *[AFP],* July 12, 1995; *[R],* July 16, 1995; *Int. Herald Tribune,* July 17, 1995; *[R], Bangkok Post,* June 22, 1994.
Like Clockwork: *Independent,* June 30, 1995; *Morning Star,* Jan. 27, 1994;

Edinburgh Eve. News, April 2, 1994; *Glasgow Herald,* Dec. 30, 1994; *Queensland Sunday Mail,* Jan. 1, 1995; *Daily Star,* Sept. 8, 1994; *Leicester Mercury,* March 6, 1995; *Sun,* June 4, 1994; *Hong Kong Stan-dard,* Dec. 9, 1994.
Against All Odds: *Daily Telegraph,* July 7, 1995; *Queensland Courier-Mail,* Jan. 20, 1995; *Sunday Express,* Oct. 16, 1994.

Prophecies   101
Star-Crossed Crossword: *Daily Tele-graph,* Sept. 23, 24, 29, 30, 1994.
Deaths Foreseen: *Lichfield & Tamworth Express & Star,* Sept. 22, 1992.
Fatal Stars: *Guardian, Independent,* Nov. 5, 1993; *Science News,* Nov. 6, 1993.
Say What?: *Daily Mirror, Sun,* Jan. 4, 1995; *Daily Star,* July 11, 1995; *Whitby Gazette,* March 24, 1994.

Apparitions   103
Tricky Dicky Rides Again: *L.A. Weekly,* Sept. 30, 1994, Oct. 6, 1994.
Ghost Plane Mystifies Postman: *Sheffield Journal,* June 1, 1995
One Dog Night Schwascar: *Edinburgh Eve. News,* June 24, 1995.
Vampire-in-Training: *Victoria* (BC) *Times-Colonist,* March 17, 24, 1993?; *[AFP],* Feb. 10, 1994; *[R],* April 11, 1994; *Times,* Sept. 13, 1994; *Rugby Observer,* Sept. 15, 1994; *Sydney Sun-Herald,* Aug. 1, 1993; *[AP],* Aug. 6, 1994.
Ghost Suspect in Bistro Blaze: *Manches-ter Evening News,* April 2, 1994.

Images   106
Nice to See Me: *Poole and Dorset Adver-tiser,* Nov. 3, 1994; *British Journal of Psychiatry,* Nov. 1994.
Fancy Meeting You Here: *[AP],* Aug. 4, 1995.
Close Family: *Bristol Eve. Post,* April 10, 1995.
Parallel Michelles: *Western Daily Press,* June 2, 1995.

Virgin Blood Floods Italy: *Catholic Herald,* March 3, 31, 1995, April 14, 1995; *Independent,* March 27, April 15, 1995; *[R],* April 14, 1995; *Daily Telegraph,* April 15, 1995; *National Enquirer,* April 18, 1995.

Medical Mishap Schwascar: *Retail Newsagent,* Feb. 18, 1995; *[AP],* March 18, 1995; *Daily Mail,* Jan. 10, 1995; *Daily Telegraph,* Feb. 18, 1995.

Tears for Vegas: *Las Vegas Weekly,* Sept. 6, 1995.

Jesus Figure Jolts Judge: *[AP], Cleveland Plain Dealer,* March 30, 1994.

Rivers of Blood: *Rocky Mountain News,* Aug. 13, 1994.

Bad Luck   111

Highway to Hell: *Wall Street Journal,* Aug. 3, 1995; *Guardian,* Aug. 7, 1995.

A Sea of Coincidence: *Times, Daily Telegraph, Independent,* Aug. 29, 1995.

Pinched Parts: *Eastbourne Herald,* May 7, 1994; *Devon Midweek Herald,* June 22, 1994; *Sun, Daily Star,* July 21, 1994.

Gift-Bearing Twins Twine Automobiles: *Sun, Independent,* Dec. 26, 1994.

Good Luck   113

The Great White Hope: *Daily Telegraph, Daily Mail,* Sept. 3, 1994; *New Scientist,* Oct. 1, 1994; *Philadelphia Inquirer,* Oct. 2, 1994, *Independent on Sunday,* Oct. 9, 1994.

Take Five: *Daily Telegraph,* Aug. 11, 1994.

Saved by the Bell: *[AP],* May 14, 1995

All in the Timing: *Sunday Mail* (Scotland), April 9, 1995; *N.Y. Times,* July 10, 1994; *People,* July 16, 1995; *[AFP],* Dec. 14, 1994; *Yorkshire Post,* Dec. 22, 1994; *Big Issue,* Jan. 25, 1995; *[R],* May 1, 1994.

Jet Boat Float: *[R, AFP],* April 7, 1995.

Musical Shopping Bags: *Canberra Times,* Dec. 7, 1994

Miracles   116

Striking Lucky: *[R],* Aug. 10, 1994; *Oxford Mail,* Aug. 11, 1994; *Guardian,* Sept. 10, 1994; *Daily Telegraph,* Sept. 16, 1994.

Baby Jesus Resurrected: *Age* (New Delhi), Nov. 22, 1994; *Daily Telegraph, Daily Mail,* Dec. 30, 1994; *Daily Mirror,* Jan. 16, 1995.

Strange Deaths: *Times, Daily Telegraph,* Feb. 13, 1995; *Today,* Dec. 28, 1993; *Birmingham Mail,* May 5, 1995; *[AP],* Aug. 1, 1995; *Today,* Aug. 2, 1995; *Le Matin* (Benin), Aug. 4, 1995; *[R],* Jan. 16; Feb. 17, 1995.

Saint's Severed Hand Provides Succor: *Hereford Times,* July 20, 1995; *Daily Telegraph,* July 22, 1995; *Times,* July 22, 24, 1995;

Cats and Dogs: *The Times, Daily Mail, Daily Record,* Jan. 3, 1995; *Jerusalem Post,* March 2, 1993; *Daily Telegraph,* June 20, 1992; *[AP],* Feb. 11; *[R],* March 4, 1995.

Poltergeists   120

Needles from Nowhere: *Heartland Evening News,* Feb. 24, 1994.

Poltergeist Girl Tragedy: *Columbus Dispatch,* May 9, 1993, Oct. 26, 1994.

Seeing is Believing: *The Big Issue,* May 3, 1994; *Independent, Daily Star,* July 2, 1994; *Daily Telegraph,* Jan. 11, 1994; *Daily Star,* Jan. 12, 1994; *Daily Telegraph,* Jan. 11, 1994; *Daily Star,* Jan. 12, 1994; *Northern Echo,* May 1993; *North Devon Journal,* June 2, 1994.

UFOs   122

Jet in Near Miss with UFO: *Manchester Eve. News,* Jan. 27, 1995; *Sun, Daily Mirror,* Jan. 28, 1995.

Chinese UFOs: *[UPI],* South China Morning Post, Aug. 9, 1995.

Official: Roswell Papers Destroyed: Press Release from Steve Schiff, July 28, 1995; *[AP],* July 29, 1995; *Times,* July 30, 1995.

Close Encounters & Alien Abductions   123

Bonnybridge Goes Intergalactic: *Glasgow Eve. Express,* Aug. 11, 1995; *Edinburgh Eve. News,* Aug. 12, 1995; *Sunday Mail,* Aug. 13, 1995; *People,* Aug. 20, 1995.

Eerie Glow in the Pacific: *[AFP],* March 25, 1995.

Head-Smacking Moves: *[AFP],* June 17, 1994; *Daily Telegraph,* Oct. 28, 1994; *New York Post,* May 10, 1995; *[AP],* Jan. 5, 1995; *USA Today,* Feb. 28, 1994.

Paranormal Experiences   125

Kangaroo Court: *Daily Telegraph,* June 8, 1995; *[R],* April 10, 1995.

Unpinning the Dragon: *[AP],* March 25, 1995.

Cab-Napper Possessed: *New Scientist,* Sept. 3, 1994; *Psychic News,* Jan. 7, 1995.

Paranormal Power Theft: *Western Mail,* Aug. 31, 1994; *Bella,* Nov. 30, 1994; *South Wales Echo,* Dec. 3, 1994.

Hoodoo that Voodoo: *Dallas Morning News,* March 24, May 27, 1994; *Independent on Sunday* (David Usborne), July 10, 1994; *[AP],* Sept. 22, 1994; *Daily Telegraph,* Sept. 23, 1994.

Archive Gems: The Hand of God: *Niagara Falls Gazette,* June 6, 1914.

Love Hurts: S. Mirror, April 14, 1991; *Daily Mirror,* Dec. 4, 1987; *Japan Times,* Aug. 15, 1993.

Bright Spark: *Sun,* March 31, 1995.

Auto-Reverse: *Southhampton Daily Echo,* May 31, 1995; *Sussex Eve. Argus,* July 22, 1995.

The Faces of Belmez : *Fortean Times* 10: 6 (June 1975); reports by Oliver Morgan in *Sunday Express,* June 4, 1995, and by Tim Brown in *Daily Telegraph,* June 5, 1995.

PHOTO CREDITS

The Human World

p. 7 *Daily Yomiuri*

p. 8 *South China Morning Post*/Max Photo

p. 10 Rex Features

p. 15 Bristol United Press

p. 17 (bottom) Dave Hogan/ Rex USA Ltd.

p. 19 Associated Press

p. 21 Joel Chant/Newsteam

p. 23 Rex USA Ltd.

p. 31 North News & Pictures

The Animal World

p. 40 (top) *Newcastle Chronicle and Journal*; (bottom) Ronald Grant Archive

p. 43 Natural History Picture Agency

p. 49 Topham Picture Point

p. 52 (top) Bob Bars; (bottom) Scotsman Publications

p. 55 Corvis-Bettmann

p. 56 Derek Briggs/University of Bristol

p. 60 Nigel Bowles/Graham Keen Agency

The Natural World

p. 69 Photo Press

p. 70 Associated Press

p. 73 UPI/Corvis-Bettmann

p. 75 Harry Taylor/British Museum

The Paranormal World

p. 98 Popperfoto/Reuters

p. 106 (top) Andy Horsfield/*Poole Advertiser*; (bottom) Associated Press

p. 108 Reuters/ANSA Romano Gentile/Archive Photos

p. 113 Steven Pazynski/Sygma

p. 116 Reuters/Pressens Bild/Archive Photos

p. 118 Newsteam International Ltd.

p. 129 Ross Parry/Rex Features